T0361744

PRAISE FOR ANNISTON RIEKSTINS AND *THE UNIVERSE IS HIRING*

"*The Universe Is Hiring* is a transformative guide that empowers readers to reconnect with their true purpose and find fulfillment beyond job titles and paychecks. By combining practical tools with spiritual insights, Anniston equips individuals to overcome internal obstacles and create a life of authentic success and joy. For anyone tired of the hustle culture and seeking deeper significance in their work, this book is a must-read. It's more than a road map; it's an invitation to transform your life from the inside out."

—**AMBERLY LAGO**, best-selling author, TEDx speaker, podcast host, coach

"I love the practical tools and advice in this book! For anyone looking to discover their purpose and find the career path that aligns with their passion, this book shows you how."

—**SARAH CENTRELLA**, #1 best-selling author of *#Futureboards*

"In a world where many are lost in the pursuit of titles and paychecks, *The Universe Is Hiring* is a guiding light. Anniston Riekstins masterfully leads readers to uncover their true purpose, showing that fulfillment isn't found in a job, but within us. This book is a must-read for anyone ready to break free from the confines of societal expectations and embrace a life of meaning and impact. It's time to stop working for a paycheck and start working for your soul."

—**KELLY SIEGEL**, host of the *Harder than Life* podcast and author of *Harder than Life*

THE UNIVERSE IS HIRING

THE UNIVERSE IS HIRING

DISCOVER THE ROLE YOU WERE BORN TO FILL

ANNISTON BLAIR RIEKSTINS

Published by Greenleaf Book Group Press
Austin, Texas
www.gbgpress.com

Distributed by Greenleaf Book Group

For ordering information or special discounts for bulk purchases, please contact Greenleaf Book Group at PO Box 91869, Austin, TX 78709, 512.891.6100.

Design and composition by Greenleaf Book Group and Sheila Parr
Cover design by Greenleaf Book Group and Sheila Parr
Cover images © Shutterstock/Mega Pixel, Paladin12, Feng Yu

Publisher's Cataloging-in-Publication data is available.

Print ISBN: 979-8-88645-259-4

eBook ISBN: 979-8-88645-260-0

To offset the number of trees consumed in the printing of our books, Greenleaf donates a portion of the proceeds from each printing to the Arbor Day Foundation. Greenleaf Book Group has replaced over 50,000 trees since 2007.

Printed in the United States of America on acid-free paper

25 26 27 28 29 30 31 32 10 9 8 7 6 5 4 3 2 1

First Edition

To my twin flame, Rudi, who stood for my vision
until I had the courage to do so.

And to Brady and Ali Olivia, who believe their mommy can do anything.

I'm starting to believe it too.

CONTENTS

INTRODUCTION

- Do you want to be more fulfilled?
- Do you long to find your purpose?
- Do you want to find a job that will be both abundant and deeply satisfying?
- Do you feel like something is missing in your life and no matter what you do, you can't seem to fill the hole inside?

IF YOU ANSWERED YES TO one or more of these questions, this book is for *you.*

What if I told you there is a specific role you—and only you—were born to fill? It exists right now and is just waiting for you to find it. One by one, your life experiences have been qualifying you to be perfectly prepared to fulfill this role. This position will require you to share your unique gifts, talents, and abilities. And it will reward you handsomely with abundance, happiness, and success beyond your wildest imagination.

If that role existed, would you be interested in applying?

I mean, who wouldn't want to be in a position that was specifically designed for them and would guarantee a lifetime of fulfillment, abundance, and happiness?

If you've picked up this book, I bet you are looking for something more in your life.

Well, I've got great news: that role does exist and it's available to you *now.*

There exists a unique role for every human on the planet. So why are so many people deeply unhappy in their careers and personal lives? Why are the rates of people living with depression, stress, and overwhelm continuing to increase? Why is suicide becoming one of the leading causes of death? Why do some of the richest, most successful people struggle with alcohol and drug addiction while claiming they still feel like something is missing?

The problem isn't that humans are *incapable* of true happiness and fulfillment. The problem is that we haven't had all the information.

In many cultures, especially in the West, we are encouraged to constantly do more: hustle harder, make more money, have more things, gain more power, and chase the impressive job title that will earn you greater respect.

We spend days, weeks, months, and years of our lives striving for these goals, sacrificing our time and happiness to survive, hoping to achieve financial freedom and enjoy life in retirement. That is, assuming that the chronic stress hasn't adversely affected our health and we live long enough to retire.

Many of us have inherited a collective belief system that includes the following:

- Life isn't meant to be easy.
- Life isn't meant to be fun.
- If an action isn't tied to a financial goal, it's a hobby and isn't as important.
- Stop dreaming, get your head out of the clouds, and return to reality.
- If you do what you love, you won't have enough money to survive.
- Keep your head down, do the work, and you'll be fine.

These beliefs have worked for centuries to ensure an individual's security, protection, and survival.

What this collective belief system doesn't support is our potential to *thrive*.

We were never taught in school how to be successful *and* fulfilled. We weren't given instructions for how to reach our dreams and feel satisfied, content, and enthusiastic every step of the way. And we're unclear how to experience true prosperity—which is the joy of doing what you were born to do while serving others and manifesting abundance at the same time.

People who perceive the world through the lens of survival are living their lives on autopilot, constantly reacting to what life throws their way. Their inner lights are dimmed, and they mindlessly go through the motions as if in a waking coma. They no longer feel excitement, joy, and love for their life; they exist and try to make the best of it until they die.

People who are thriving seem to glow from the inside out. They wake up excited about what the day will bring and spend time doing the things that light them up. They dream about their future and intentionally create their heart's desires. These people have magnetic energy and are invigorating to be around. And no matter where they go, they experience beautiful synchronicities that could easily be perceived as luck, as if everything they touch turns to gold.

Let me ask you: Are you surviving or are you thriving? Your answer will determine the quality of the life you will experience, and it's a choice.

If you're not currently thriving, the good news is that it's more than possible for you to shift into that state. But it will require you to stop doing what you've been taught—expecting money, relationships, jobs, and all sorts of material objects to fill your inner cup.

Because this invisible cup can only be filled by one thing, and that is your *purpose*.

I discovered and aligned with my purpose in my early thirties, creating a significant turning point in my life story. It changed *everything*.

I know what it feels like to be deeply unfulfilled, suffering in silence, feeling like your job is sucking the life force out of you. I know what it feels like to job-hop, believing with each new job that you've finally found a position that will keep you feeling inspired, fulfilled, and engaged, only to feel dissatisfied again a year later. I know what it feels like to come home from work and feel like you have nothing to give your spouse and children because your energy tank is perpetually empty. I know what it feels like to fall into a deep depression every Sunday evening, knowing Monday morning and a full calendar of meetings are right around the corner. I know what it feels like to have no idea what you're good at and to feel deeply unworthy of success. And I know what it feels like to be constantly searching for a purpose, wondering why others seem so sure of themselves while you feel lost.

I've been there, and it sucks. Especially when you have achieved everything you believed was necessary—the career, marriage, mortgage, children, and 401k—but it's still not enough.

Nothing was enough until I did the inner work to discover, align with, and start *being* my purpose. I will share my journey and process with you throughout the following pages, but know that it led to me creating and living a life I love.

I discovered that it's possible to *have it all*, and I have designed and crafted a life that lights me up.

Today, I serve as a high-level executive for a large, ever-expanding company. I absolutely love my job and the incredible humans I'm blessed to work with. In addition to my job function, I regularly host training workshops for the company, teaching employees how to release limiting beliefs and bring more meaning to their work by connecting to their unique purpose.

My husband, Rudi Riekstins, is a high-performance coach who supports companies to elevate their leadership and overall culture. Together, we host *The InPowered Life* podcast and co-founded InPower University, an online platform offering transformational digital courses and coaching.

Writing is my passion, so I fill my cup most mornings between 4 a.m. and 6 a.m. writing books like the one you hold now. My crowning achievement is the honor of being a mother to my two brilliant and beautiful children, Brady and Ali Olivia.

You might wonder how it's possible to have a demanding job and home life and still make time for passions like writing, podcasting, and coaching. Yes, my life is incredibly full. I have intentionally filled my plate to the very edges with *only* what is aligned with my values and overall purpose. I've designed a life that fully reflects my authentic self, and the result is that I'm happy and fulfilled.

My journey to the purposeful life I now enjoy was long, winding, and messy. But I learned a lot and am now passionate about sharing this message with the world in any way I can.

The Universe Is Hiring is a call to step forward into living and expressing your unique purpose. It's a love note from the Universe reminding you that you are a one-of-a-kind, limited edition, never-to-be-replicated human being, and you came here to do something big.

It's a wake-up call to get you out of sleepwalking through your life so you can remember and start living your heroic mission.

It's a guide, pointing you down the path that will lead to everything you seek—abundance, fulfillment, joy, passion, and love.

I've divided this book into four parts.

Part 1 guides you toward taking accountability for your life, reconnecting with your authentic self, and defining your unique purpose, and it shows you how to manifest your most important dreams and desires.

Part 2 addresses the standard roadblocks you will encounter when expressing your purpose in the world, including your fears, limiting beliefs, imposter syndrome, and comparison. These chapters provide self-awareness and tools you can use to break through the obstacles when they appear.

Part 3 is where the road map to aligning with your purpose begins. It guides you through the process I used and have taught to thousands of others. You'll learn to start where you are, take inspired action, commit to your desires, surrender, and let go of the outcome.

Finally, Part 4 includes tips on embodying this new way of being and not falling back into old habitual patterns of survival-living. I guide you to trust your heart and feel your way forward, rather than relying solely on your logical thinking mind. I also teach you how to reframe your fears about money and encourage you to become a student of life so you can continue to grow, evolve, and expand into even greater versions of yourself.

It's important to note that this book is not written for or against any one religion or belief system. I believe there are many paths to God, Source, Chi, the Universe, or whatever you want to call the creator of all that is. For this book, I've chosen to use the words "Universe" and "Source," but know that I honor and respect each of you and the journey you have chosen to connect with your creator. This book reflects the qualities we *all* share, not the beliefs that often serve to separate us.

Here's the truth: Nothing will change in your life until you do.

If you commit to joining me on the journey in the following chapters, you will make changes in the only place you can—and that's within.

Suppose you take just one recommendation from this book and implement it. In doing so, you will forever alter the trajectory of your life. Knowledge isn't powerful until you do something with it, so applying what you learn is crucial.

At the end of each chapter, you'll notice a section called "Putting it into practice." In this section, I provide at least one action step, exercise, or thought starter that you can put into action so you can anchor the information. Experience is the most outstanding teacher, so you need to create time to do the work intentionally.

The immediate benefit of doing this work is that you will feel lighter, happier, more hopeful, and excited about the future you are creating. Then, as you continue implementing the practices given, your external world will shift in small and massive ways.

My students and coaching clients have experienced new job opportunities, promotions, raises, launching new businesses, connecting with soul mates, getting married, moving across the country, buying dream homes, feeling balanced and calm, getting off anxiety medication, repairing broken relationships, landing book deals, and so much more.

It's no longer enough to *know* that you have a purpose—you must know how to align with and embody it. This book is a guide to help you do just that.

I'm honored to play a part in your journey. Your life matters, and there's something you are here to do. Don't waste another day not living your best, most authentic, purposeful life.

Let's get started.

Part 1

CLARIFY YOUR VISION

Chapter 1

TAKE THE WHEEL

The moment you take responsibility for everything in your life is the moment you can change anything in your life.

—Hal Elrod, Author and Creator of The Miracle Morning Method

I'M HONORED AND EXCITED TO begin this journey with you. Your decision to read this book indicates that you want *more* out of life than you're getting now, and you believe you deserve it. The fact that you're reading this page means there is something for you to learn here—something that might be that next step, or giant leap, toward creating a better life.

As appealing as it can be to jump right into the fun parts of clarifying your unique purpose and experiencing a new, improved version of you, we can't skip one critical step. First, you must turn around and look back to figure out *how you got here*. And I'm not talking about how you arrived on this planet. I'm referring to the millions of thoughts, choices, and actions that ultimately got you to where you are today, living the life experience you find yourself in *now.*

You can only take charge of manifesting the future you desire if you're willing to take accountability for the life you created up until now. Think about it: How will you ever believe you can make real change in your life if you never admit that *you* played the most significant part in creating the life you have now?

Before passing GO, you must take full accountability and responsibility for *yourself.*

Let's start by investigating your past. If you don't start there, you are likely to unconsciously re-create the same patterns, behaviors, and outcomes that got you where you are today. Your history also holds beautiful breadcrumbs—your soul's clues—that will help you identify the path that will bring you the most joy, fulfillment, and success.

Let's take a few minutes to self-reflect. I recommend grabbing a pen and paper as you answer the following questions. Also, it's important to note this is a self-*assessment,* not an excuse to dive into the hole of blame, shame, and despair. It's important to answer honestly.

What you're willing to hide, you get to keep. What you're brave enough to name, you get to *reframe.*

- How are you feeling right now? What's your dominant emotional state?
- On a scale of 1 to 10, how would you rate the quality of your life?
- How would you rate the quality of your relationships?
- What dreams and desires have you yet to achieve?
- What experiences in your past still cause you pain (physical, mental, emotional)?
- What regrets and resentments do you carry?
- Are you happy with your life, or do you feel there is room for improvement?

If you answered the questions, I'm proud of you. It takes courage to peer into the mirror of your life. If you decided this exercise wasn't essential and skipped right to this paragraph, I implore you to reconsider and at least contemplate these questions. As the late, great Dr. Wayne Dyer said, "If you don't make peace with your past, it will keep showing up in your present."

Your past is an anchor keeping you in place, and to pull it up you have to examine, reframe, and release what no longer serves you. What I love about this analogy is the anchor didn't put itself in the water—you consciously or unconsciously threw it in. And whether you let it hold you back from sailing to different waters is, again, *up to you.*

It's important to note that healing past wounds and traumas is a process. For some, it will require seeking help from a mental health professional, therapist, or doctor. You might start on this journey of self-reflection and realize it's too daunting to go it alone, and there's no shame in that. Many have supported my healing and growth, and I have in turn supported others. Seek out the help you need. You and your happiness are worth it.

I will guide you toward pulling up that heavy anchor of your past and setting sail for serene, abundant waters. You're the only one who can change your life, and it starts by owning up to the part you've played in creating your life up until now.

HOW DID YOU GET HERE?

How did you arrive in the place you're sitting right now?

Let's pretend I gave you a DVD of your life until now and told you to watch it in one sitting, from start to finish. You observe *yourself,* the main character of this epic film, processing life from a specific point of view, responding to situations, making decisions, taking necessary actions, starting and leaving relationships, and behaving in positive and negative ways. From this spectator's seat, you would see that your life up until now is the sum total of all your choices.

Did you turn left or right, accept or decline the job offer, stay in the relationship or leave, move to the new city, believe in yourself, say yes to the opportunity or not, spend the money or save? How did you choose to feel about an experience, and based on that feeling, what actions did you take? Did you decide to forgive or hold on to old resentments? Did you overcome the fear holding you back or avoid dealing with it?

Every choice you have made has led you down a path. If you could zoom far enough out, you would see millions of potential paths you could've taken, each veering off the other based on your choices, moment to moment. It's overwhelming to think about.

Let me teach you a simple formula for life: *You + Your Choices = Life Outcome.*

In this formula, you and the choices you do or don't make are ultimately your life's cause and effect. In another chapter, we dive into *why* you make your choices based on your belief system and unconscious programs. However, you ultimately still decide how you will think, feel, act, and behave.

In my experience, I've found that many individuals believe their life formula looks more like this: *Me + My Parents + My Ex-husband + The Job I Hate + Not Enough Money + Chronic Health Issues + Ungrateful Children = Life Outcome.*

Just writing this example makes me feel *disempowered.* As appealing as it can be to blame other people and circumstances for our lives, it's also depressing because if this formula were true, it would mean we have no control over our life experiences.

You can live an entire life (and many do) blaming everyone and everything for how you feel, how much money you have, staying in a job you hate, and giving up on your dreams. Or, you can take full accountability and responsibility for your life and get busy creating what you want.

Depending on your choice, you will live as a victim or a victor.

VICTIM VS. VICTOR

You can't play both the *victim* and *victor* in the great movie of your life—you have to choose.

Let's dig into each character so you can make an informed decision about who you want to be.

Victims view their life as though it is happening *to* them, creating their dominant state of being, mindset, and attitude toward life. The victim doesn't know how to take accountability for anything in their life because their prevailing belief is "How could it be my fault if I have no control over my life?" They will tell the story of how hard life is, believing there are unmovable obstacles standing in the way of them ever achieving their goals. They think they have been dealt an unfair hand while everyone else seems to be magically bestowed with an abundance of love, success, and happiness.

Now let's look at my favorite character to play—the *victor*. Victors believe life is happening *for* them and take full accountability for their life experience. The victor perceives life's challenges and obstacles as blessings and necessary catalysts for growth. They understand failure is learning and an essential step toward success. A victor spends more time reflecting on their actions and behaviors than making excuses, blaming, and complaining when they don't like the outcome. They build solid and healthy relationships because they don't expect their loved ones to make them feel happy, fulfilled, and successful. They have created a positive belief system that supports overcoming the fears and limiting beliefs that would otherwise hold them back from sharing their gifts and fulfilling their destiny. The victor isn't interested in just surviving—they are committed to *thriving*.

So, which character are you? And more importantly, which one do you *want to be*?

There are an infinite number of paths before you, and each will lead to a different experience—abundant, lacking, fulfilling, soul-sucking, joyful, challenging, and triumphant beyond your wildest imagination. So, how do you make sure you're choosing the *best* path? A good start is ensuring you select and develop the most supportive mindset. It's time to become the victor of your life, the great hero or heroine of your story.

I adore this quote from John C. Maxwell, American author and orator: "The greatest day in your life and mine is when we take total responsibility for our attitudes. That's the day we truly grow up." Let today be *the day* you decide to radically change your life for the better.

I acknowledge that some of you have experienced unthinkable traumas, abuse, neglect, poverty, chronic pain, loss, and disease. And it's part of our culture to refer to individuals who have experienced these challenges as *victims.* But as American singer and actress Naomi Judd once said, "You're only a victim once. After that, you're a volunteer."

While you probably didn't consciously *choose* to have that experience, you can decide how you will let that experience affect and define you. You take your power back and become the victor when you stop looking at life's challenges as something you must *go* through and start perceiving them as something you can *grow* through.

LET GO OF VICTIM BEHAVIOR

People don't tell you who they are—they *show you*. Your behavior exposes your unconscious beliefs, thoughts, and feelings. The following common behaviors are symptoms of a victim mentality.

Blaming

Have you ever noticed that when blaming, you're focused externally on another person or experience?

Blaming is an avoidance of taking responsibility for your part in what happened. It's saying, "I have no power in this situation." Once, I received an angry email from a client because someone on my team had failed to communicate proper timelines, which would negatively impact an upcoming launch of a new product. My initial reaction was anger and disappointment in my team member for dropping the ball—mainly because it made *me* look bad. But then, as I calmed myself down, I asked the question, "What did I do to contribute to this outcome?"

I could have followed up with the manager to ensure she had communicated expectations and timelines to the client. I could have made sure she fully understood the project and my expectations. I had made assumptions that she understood the proper steps to take, and those assumptions were the cause of this breakdown in communication. It was *my* fault.

I scheduled a call with the client and explained what had happened, taking full responsibility, and then shared what I had learned and the measures I would take to ensure this didn't happen again. I could've reacted angrily and pointed the finger at my direct report—but then I would've robbed myself of invaluable learning and growth.

Suppose you blame others for how your life has turned out. In that case, you're missing the golden opportunity to see your part in contributing to that outcome and to learn from your mistakes. And from that learning, you will make different choices in the future. The people who choose to blame will continue to repeat the same negative patterns. Challenges, obstacles, and perceived failures are your most incredible growth opportunities, but only when you're willing to stop pointing and use all of those fingers to grab a *mirror.*

Complaining

Complaining is a common condition of the human race. We emotionally connect with others who have similar complaints, like how busy we are or how difficult it is to be a parent. We fill awkward, quiet moments in the elevator or before a meeting starts with complaints about things we have no control over, like the weather. I mean, what a hilarious waste of time.

If you doubt how conditioned you are to complain, I challenge you to go twenty-four hours without complaining to anyone about anything. While you might fail, this exercise will open your eyes to how unconscious you are of the words you speak aloud.

As Jack Canfield wrote in *The Success Principles: How to Get from Where You Are to Where You Want to Be,* "Complaining is an ineffective response to an event that does not produce a better outcome."

How often have you complained to your best friend about your spouse's inability to communicate or your resentment over them not helping more with the kids? While it might give you temporary relief to speak your grievances out loud, your best friend isn't going to fix your issues with your partner. The only person who can do that is *you* and your *partner.*

So why not go to the source? Because it takes courage to speak your truth. It takes guts to risk rocking the boat with your partner, colleague, or best friend. So we take the easy way out and complain about it, often to people with no stake in the situation or power to create a change.

Complaining is a victim behavior caused by a limiting belief that what you want doesn't matter or that it's not safe to speak your truth. I recommend you push through the uncomfortable fears; the more you do, the easier it becomes.

Excuses

Remember the last time you botched a task, made a mistake, or experienced a perceived failure. Did you take full responsibility for the outcome? Or did you spend time and energy creating a comprehensive list of all the external reasons you failed?

I almost bailed on completing this book.

Why, you ask?

I had a laundry list of excuses that I would've happily shared with you—I got promoted to vice president, and with it came more responsibility and a full calendar; I couldn't write in the mornings because the kids needed my help getting ready for school; I wasn't feeling creatively inspired; I hadn't studied the topic enough and it required more research; I didn't get enough sleep; the house was too loud for me to concentrate; my eye wouldn't stop twitching; my stomach was growling. My excuses were so good that even I started believing them.

One day, my husband Rudi asked me why I had stopped writing. I held my head high as I listed all my excuses, feeling confident I would convince him of the *impossibility* of completion. He saw right through my bullshit.

Rudi responded, "Be that as it may, what would it take for you to complete and publish this book?" Damn, he had me right where he wanted me. None of my excuses were insurmountable; in fact, they were utter crap. I didn't have a leg to stand on, so I let go of the "it's impossible" story I had concocted and instead created an action plan.

I adjusted my sleep schedule so I could wake up at 4:30 a.m., which allowed me two hours to write before the kids needed to get up for school. I carried a notebook with me during the day to write down ideas when I felt creatively inspired. I prepared the coffee pot every evening, so I was assured not to waste time in the morning. I also created accountability partners by sharing my intention to complete this book with several colleagues and family members.

When I stopped wasting energy coming up with excuses, I could direct that energy to create something that has since brought me unbelievable fulfillment and joy. It's the gift that keeps on giving, as I know it will impact many lives, not just my own.

Your excuses are like thieves in the night, silently stealing the time, energy, and resources you need to achieve the desires of your heart. Holding on to your excuses will never move you forward, but it will ensure you stay exactly where you are. Excuses are an unconscious response to fear of failure, fear of success, and fear of the unknown. And with every excuse you make, there is an opportunity cost.

What are your excuses costing you? They are costing you the highest, best, most potent, and most successful version of yourself. They are costing you feelings of joy, abundance, and love. They are costing you the knowing that you are unlimited and capable of achieving anything you desire.

You need to adopt a new rule: no excuses.

If you hit a snag, problem, or roadblock, ask yourself the question Rudi asked me: What would it take for you to move forward and succeed? Bypass the need for excuses, and momentum will carry you toward your desired destination.

Now that you are fully aware of the disempowering behaviors that will keep you living life as a victim, you are perfectly poised to catch yourself in the act and change your behavior.

As the famous American poet, memoirist, and civil rights activist Maya Angelou is reported to have said to her friend Oprah Winfrey, "You did what you knew how to do, and when you knew better, you did better."

THE GREAT REWRITE

You are the author of your life story, which also means you have final editing rights. Looking back at your life, do you see how every moment and decision supported you in becoming the person you are today and who you will become in the future? Or is your story a tragedy that moves from one moment of despair to another, never to reach a happily ever after?

I once supported a client in rewriting her story, and doing so radically changed her life. On her first coaching call, tears poured down her cheeks as she spoke of one terrible experience after another. She was in a horrific car accident that left her with chronic pain; her husband left her; she lost her job; she became estranged from her kids; and, to make matters worse, she was diagnosed with cancer. I mean, *wow*.

After thanking her for sharing, I gave her an assignment for the next call. She would tell me her story again in two weeks, but this time from an empowered perspective. She would have to seek the blessing in all her most challenging experiences, what she had learned, and how they had been necessary for her growth. She looked at me like I was insane, but she reluctantly agreed.

As promised, she showed up ready to go on her second call. She had written page after page of her life story from the perspective of power and gratitude. To my surprise, she *looked* and *sounded* like a different person. The defeated, weak, sad woman of two weeks before had been replaced with a confident, beautiful, shining teacher who had *so* much wisdom to share. Again, she had tears running down her cheeks, but this time she was crying with relief, knowing that all of the challenging moments had a purpose; for the first time in a very long time, she felt *hope*.

She realized that playing the victim had gotten her sympathy from others, negative attention, and excuses to remain stuck—but all of it came at the cost of her healing, happiness, and freedom from past pain.

When you can assign purpose and meaning to your past, it prepares you to find meaning in your present. You're constantly being prepared for what is next as you grow into the person you're meant to be.

Let's look at your career. What's the purpose of your current job? What skills are you learning? What people are you interacting with and affecting daily? What talents and skills do you rely on now that you learned in a previous job? And what is this job *preparing* you for?

I don't believe in accidents or wasted moments. *Everything* has a purpose in your life. Otherwise, it wouldn't be there. Your job is to seek out the meaning in each moment, and by doing so, you'll start to see and feel the beautiful, intelligent, universal energy that is guiding you toward your destiny.

You will feel better when you stop resisting what is and trust that you are where you are for a reason. What you resist persists, but when you can come to a place of acceptance, you open yourself up to the next opportunity.

If you take full accountability for your life and make peace with your past and present, a beautiful doorway will open within your heart. If you listen, you'll hear a quiet voice saying, "This is the way."

PUTTING IT INTO PRACTICE

I challenge you to write your empowered story.

1. Grab your journal and pen.
2. List five or six of the most challenging, emotionally heightened moments from your past.
3. Next to each one, take accountability for that situation:
   - What was your part in it?
   - What did you learn and gain from each of those situations?
   - How did that situation impact who you are today?
   - How has that experience allowed you to impact and serve others?
4. Write out the aspects of your life you are unhappy with right now. Next to each one, write out what you're learning and gaining from each situation. If it helps, pretend you are three years in the future,

having already achieved your desired success. What did you gain from the experience you're in now? Why was it such an important stepping stone?

5. When it's complete, read your new story aloud to yourself (and if you feel comfortable, share it with someone you love and trust). Notice how you feel in your body when you look at your life through the lens of your empowered story. Do you notice a positive shift in how you perceive yourself and your life?

Chapter 2

REVISE YOUR RESUME

Discover your divinity, find your unique
talent, serve humanity with it.
—Deepak Chopra, Indian American Author
and Alternative Medicine Advocate

WHAT IF THE UNIVERSE POSTED an ad for a job specifically designed for you, the role you were born to fill? Would you recognize it? Would you see the list of qualities and skills required and think, *This is a role I'm uniquely qualified for*? And if you did, would you feel worthy and capable enough to apply?

In this chapter, I re-introduce you to a significant person who will be with you every step of this journey. This individual's guidance will help you align with your purpose and experience consistent fulfillment, joy, and success. In fact, without their assistance, your mission will most certainly fail.

This person is *you.*

Let me clarify: This individual is not the mask you wear—the character that has been molded and developed since childhood and is deemed acceptable by your family, friends, and community—the person you might believe yourself to be.

I'm referring to your *authentic* self—the version of you that is unique, natural, real, and reflects your one-of-a-kind design, created by the source of all that is.

According to renowned author and spiritual teacher Eckhart Tolle, "Only the truth of who you are, if realized, will set you free." The great turning point in your life's story happens when you stop avoiding, denying, and running from your true self and take the time to get to know the real you underneath the costume you wear.

If you don't know who you are, how can you know what you want, which direction to take, or what to pursue? How can you choose the best job, relationships, hobbies, and experiences that will make you feel happy instead of more lost and unfulfilled?

I have heard hundreds, if not thousands, of clients, friends, and colleagues say, "I don't know what I'm good at. I don't know what I should do with my life. I don't know what my purpose is."

And here's what I say in response: "Congratulations! You're ready."

Why? Because when you start asking the right questions, you're ready to receive the answers.

Have you ever noticed that some people seem blissfully unaware that they are miserable in the life they have created for themselves and they never stop to question why they feel this way or what they can do to change it? And any intervention or prompting on your part only pisses them off? It's because they're *not ready.*

I would bet if you're reading this book, *you're ready.*

In my experience, there comes a point in your life where you start to question who you are and your life's choices. What you thought were important priorities no longer feel that way. No amount of money will give you the fulfillment you seek. Neither will nice clothes, expensive sports cars, or beautiful companions. You realize you worked so hard to fill your life with all the external things—job titles, relationships, and experiences you believed were the *way to eternal happiness*—only to find you're still left with an unfillable hole inside.

That hole can only be filled by *being your true self* and fulfilling your purpose.

But how do you do that? How do you course correct after spending so many years creating a life that doesn't feel authentic? The ancient Greek philosopher Socrates spoke to this question many moons ago when he said, "Know thyself."

The road back to your authentic self can be long and challenging, or it can happen in an instant.

I spent most of my teens and twenties feeling insecure, lost, and unsure of what to do with my life. No one knew how I felt because I wore a carefully crafted mask of a self-assured, independent, and successful young woman. Deep down, I didn't want to acknowledge to anyone—especially myself—that I didn't know who I was, what I was good at, or what I wanted for my life. Essentially, I didn't know *why* I was here.

Fast-forward a decade. I was married to my soulmate, expecting our first child, and in a great job. Everything in my life was perfect on paper. I had achieved the American dream and had the marriage certificate, mortgage, bank account, and baby bump to prove it. Everything was *fine*—except for me.

I felt like a massive imposter in my own life, and I was terrified of anyone discovering the insecure, weak, mediocre person I was at my core. I didn't feel worthy of the man who loved me, talented enough to succeed in my career, smart enough to create financial wealth, or loving enough to raise children.

So, I made it my mission to *be* what everyone wanted me to be—this way, they would never know the truth. I was a chameleon, changing my colors to suit whomever I was in the moment. I was the perfect wife, an ideal and agreeable employee who always said and did the *right* thing, and a lovely friend who would always tell you what you wanted to hear. I wanted to make everyone happy, and I felt safe as long as they felt comfortable.

This strategy worked until the unease and unfulfillment of my youth bubbled to the surface. I had everything I wanted, but it wasn't enough. I couldn't blame it on anything outside myself because I had everything I thought I wanted, so I was forced to examine the one place I had avoided my entire life: my inner world of emotion and feeling.

I began to peer into the negative emotions and ask the right questions. Who am I? What are my unique talents and gifts? What are my authentic dreams and desires? What do I need to let go of? What brings me joy? Why do I feel unfulfilled?

My answers to these questions were eye-opening. They disrupted my habitual thinking and opened the first of many cracks in the false identity I had created.

My inner turmoil, unease, and unfulfillment were the most significant catalysts for my spiritual growth and development. The inward journey led to rediscovering who I was at my core—my heart and soul.

From this vantage point, I could more clearly see and accept my unique gifts, genuine interests, strengths, growth areas, beauty, depth, wisdom, and ability to love.

This profound aha moment was a positive turning point in my story. Once I knew who I was, I started making decisions that reflected what I wanted, not what I thought I *should* want. I started honoring what brought me joy, allowing that to guide me.

I prioritized spending time honing my natural gifts because doing so lit me up. I took my power back, knowing I could make changes that would make me feel better in my life. I felt excited and hopeful about my future, as I believed that my natural desires were not only given to me for a reason but also were within my ability to achieve.

My inner light shone brightly for all to see, lighting my way forward.

Are you showing up and unapologetically expressing your authentic self? Are you living a life that reflects your inner desires—not those of your family, friends, or community? Are your days filled with "I want to" or, even better, "I get to," instead of "I should"?

Or do you have some work to do to realign with your most authentic self?

YOUR AUTHENTIC SELF

According to bestselling author and philanthropist Sarah Ban Breathnach, "The authentic self is the soul made visible." It's the raw, undiluted, unhidden version of you. No masks. No costumes.

Authenticity is the courage to be yourself. And it does take courage because we live in a world that celebrates conformity and discourages being different. If we were all meant to be the same, don't you think we would all be born with the *same* physical bodies, thoughts, dreams, desires, and perspectives on life? What a ridiculous, boring world that would be.

You are one of a kind. There will *never* be another you. So, if you don't show up to be you in this lifetime, no one else will. No replacements are waiting on the sidelines. If you don't recognize, master, and share your unique gifts with the world, the life puzzle will never be complete—as it'll be missing the perfectly shaped piece that is you.

What if your unique gift will be the answer to one of the world's significant issues? What if the song you create lifts someone's spirit when they need it most? What if your inspired idea positively changes the way we live? What if your gift of teaching catalyzes one of your students to reach for more in their life?

Don't you see? You matter more than you will ever comprehend. We are all connected, and your contribution to the world is imperative. You shouldn't be anyone but yourself. As the saying goes, "Be yourself; everyone else is already taken."

Authenticity is found at the intersection of who you are and what you do—when you *do* who you *are*.

Expressing the real you is the equivalent of plugging into your higher power. It allows you to experience the elevated emotions you seek—gratitude, fulfillment, joy, and love.

So, why would you choose *not* to be your authentic self?

Because at some point in your life—probably early childhood—you formed the belief that your natural passions, talents, dreams, and desires were not significant and didn't matter. You then were told—or witnessed—the physical appearance, qualities, skills, and talents valued by your family, friends, community, and culture. You compartmentalized and packed away the parts of yourself you believed unacceptable and started to pretend to be the person you thought you should be to be accepted by the tribe, survive, and succeed in life. Eventually, after playing this character long enough, you forgot you were pretending and believed this to be who you were.

The long-term effects of being someone you're not and living a life that isn't natural or meant for you can lead to physical disease, mental health issues, and a horrible life experience.

SIGNS YOU ARE *NOT BEING* YOUR AUTHENTIC SELF

You must be able to self-diagnose when you're out of alignment with your authentic self. What follows are a few common symptoms.

1. **You feel unhappy.**
   This symptom encompasses a bevy of negative emotions including feeling stressed-out, depressed, anxious, overwhelmed, lackluster, hopeless, and uninspired. It can feel like you're off or out of sorts, but you can't pinpoint why.

2. **You seek validation from others.**
   You feel your worth is connected to and controlled by others' approval, compliments, or the number of likes you get on your Instagram post. And if, for some reason, you aren't receiving these things, you start to question yourself and your value. Feeling this way also makes it hard to make decisions that aren't accepted by those you are looking to for validation.

3. **You let others make decisions for you.**
   You trust the opinions and advice of others over your own intuition and feelings. Because you don't know who you are, making decisions can be difficult, so rather than make a mistake, you follow someone else's guidance, believing they know better than you.

4. **You compromise your values.**
   You find yourself doing things you never thought you would—lying, cheating, gossiping, stealing, and not acting with integrity.

5. **You feel tired.**
   Living disconnected from your authentic self is the equivalent of draining your phone battery and wondering why it won't turn on in the morning. You not only feel physically drained but also mentally and emotionally spent. Trying to be someone you're not will zap every ounce of energy you have, and no amount of sleep will make you feel better.

SIGNS YOU ARE *BEING* YOUR AUTHENTIC SELF

Just as you need to know when you're out of alignment, it's essential to know when you're aligned. In my experience, the fantastic feeling of *being* my authentic self is my sign. Still, a few other behaviors indicate that you're on the right path.

1. **Your life is an expression of your values.**
   You know what's important to you, and that's what you invest your energy, time, finances, and resources into. You honor that everyone has different values, and rather than judging, you focus on staying true to your own.

2. **You have healthy boundaries.**
   You remain compassionate and empathetic while honoring your needs, wants, and desires. You can communicate clearly with your loved ones what you're willing to do and what you're not. You also choose to spend time with those who fill you up, not drain you dry.

3. **You honor what feels right to you.**
   You trust your inner compass and act when it feels right. While you might ask for feedback and advice, your opinion matters most. And when you feel inspired, you're willing to take the road less traveled and march to the beat of your own drum.

4. **You're self-aware and you continue to grow.**
   You know your strengths and weaknesses and love yourself enough to invest in up-leveling your mindset, learning new skills, and trying new things. You are compassionate and patient with yourself, understanding that there is no destination, just more learning.

5. **You value your gifts and look for ways to share them with the world.**
   You know your unique gifts, honor their value and importance, spend time honing them, and actively look for ways to share them with those around you. You feel the joy from getting lost in your craft and find that life flows more easily when you do what you love.

There are so many benefits to aligning with and expressing your authentic self. The biggest one is the ability to experience the absolute best, most talented, influential, and happiest version of yourself.

I believe that when you're authentic, you *glow* from the inside out.

This beautiful light magnetizes others to you, even if they don't understand why—they want what you have. You become a magnet to synchronicities and miraculous events that move you forward and expand your ability to share your gifts and create abundance.

DISCOVER YOUR AUTHENTIC SELF

Are you ready to align with your beautiful, powerful, authentic self?

I've got good and bad news: The good news is that only you can discover who you are. The bad news is that only *you* can discover who you are.

No hack, software, Google search, book, course, teacher, or expert can tell you who you are and what you should do.

Have you ever created a resume? The traditional resume lists all of your work experience and the skills and abilities you have that are relevant to the job you are applying for. When I interview candidates for management positions in our company, I ask for information that is not listed on their resume:

What lights you up? What is your zone of genius? What is your hidden talent? What are your best qualities? Where are your areas of growth?

I want to know the *real* version of the candidate, not the mask. If I can hire people who are naturally good at or passionate about the job function, they will not only perform at a much higher level, they will also be happy, and they'll stick around.

How would my life have been different if, before launching down a career path, I had *first* created a resume reflective of my authentic self? How would that soul-inspired CV have informed and guided my way forward? It would have changed *a lot.*

Rudi and I developed a powerful exercise we share with our coaching clients, and I will share it with you. You're going to create a one-page Authentic Self Resume.

This document reflects your true identity, what you want, and your unique purpose. It should evolve as you continue to grow and change. This resume acts as a guide to ensure you are remaining true to yourself, especially when you're feeling fear and uncertainty.

PUTTING IT INTO PRACTICE

How do you start? By creating the time and space to ask yourself—and contemplate the answers to—some critical questions. When you start asking better questions, you will gain new insights about yourself. Questions are also the best way to cut through your habitual belief system and disrupt the opinions about yourself that you're perceiving as facts.

Grab a journal and write the following questions, or head to www.anistonriekstins.com to download, print, and complete the **Discover Your Authentic Self** questionnaire. Please take your time with this exercise.

- What did you love to do as a child? (What were your hobbies and interests?)

- What subjects, sports, and activities came easy to you?
- What were your unique personality traits?
- What do you love most about yourself?
- What do you not like about yourself?
- What are your core values? (What's most important to you?)
- What kind of activities are you naturally drawn to?
- What gives you energy?
- What drains you of energy?
- What do you want more of?
- What do you need to let go of?
- What fears and limiting beliefs hinder you from living your desired life?
- What topics are you extremely knowledgeable about?
- What do people come to you for? (On what topics or in what events do they seek your advice, support, direction?)
- When do you experience losing time (i.e., getting lost or feeling in flow) while doing something?
- What would you do for others for free?
- What does the best version of yourself look like?
- How would someone who loves you describe you to a stranger?
- What are you most proud of yourself for? Your biggest accomplishment?
- What do you want to be remembered for?

Next, it's time to condense the information you've discovered into the following categories. Find a clean page in your journal or download the **Authentic Self Resume** document from www.annistonriekstins.com resources and complete the following sentences.

- My passions are . . .

- My natural skills and talents are . . .
- What brings me joy is . . .
- What's important to me is . . .
- What I have learned from my past experiences is . . .
- My unique superpower is . . .
- I serve others by . . .
- My vision for my life is . . .

When you do the work, you get the reward.

The work of reconnecting with my authentic self has produced the most significant rewards of my life. I finally felt *at home* within myself and the life I was creating. I experienced what true peace, joy, and fulfillment felt like.

When I began honoring my uniqueness and developing my natural gifts, I felt *worthy* of love, success, and happiness. And when I allowed inner joy to guide me to do the things that lit me up, my entire world transformed.

Ultimately, the greatest reward was falling in love with *myself*.

If you were sitting in front of me right now, I would take your hand, look you in the eye, and say the following:

You are worth the effort.

You deserve to live a life you love.

You have unique talents to share.

Your life matters.

I love you.

Don't waste another precious day not knowing who you are.

You do *you*.

Chapter 3

DISCOVER YOUR PURPOSE

The two most important days in life are the day you were born and the day you discover the reason why.

—Anonymous

IT'S NOT ENOUGH.

You've tried your hardest to create your best life, yet something within you wants more—an inner, unquenchable thirst.

I was speaking to Paige, one of my dear friends from college, catching up on life, when she stopped the pleasantries and shared what was really going on. "Anniston, I'm struggling. I'm a forty-year-old woman who has worked hard to build my career and succeeded. But I'm not happy. I have felt dissatisfied for a while but assumed it was because I hadn't yet reached the job title I wanted. However, now I'm a vice president of my organization, and it's still not enough. What's wrong with me? When does it ever get to be enough? I feel like I'm supposed to be doing more with my life. I want the work I do every day to be more meaningful and useful in the world, but I can't figure out what my purpose is, no matter how hard I try."

I admired Paige's courage to speak aloud what so many people are ashamed to admit. She felt guilty for wanting more and confused because she didn't know what "more" was. I bet you've had a similar experience to Paige at some point in your life, *or* you're experiencing it now.

I am so passionate about this topic because I've been there. For years, I experienced feelings of shame, guilt, frustration, and confusion related to my career—wanting to find the purpose and meaning in what I was doing beyond increasing a corporation's bottom line and taking home a paycheck.

That is until I discovered and started living my purpose—a story I share later in this chapter.

You should *never* feel guilty about wanting more for yourself. Guilt is one of the most destructive, toxic emotions in the human spectrum. It's not our inner urge to seek more fulfillment in life that needs to change—it's our beliefs, perceptions, and attitude toward expansion that require reconsideration.

Did you know the nature of the Universe is *expansion*? Science shows that the Universe hasn't stopped expanding since the beginning of time. You are made by the same source that created the Universe, so it would make sense that you, too, are made of the same expansive energy. To expand is to continue to grow, evolve, and change. It's completely natural. What is *unnatural* is to stay the same.

If you felt 100 percent satisfied with your life just as it is, you wouldn't have the urge to seek experiences that would act as the catalyst for your next level of growth and expansion. So, your deep desire to have, be, and do something more with your life is normal and healthy.

Furthermore, neuroscience shows that it's not the achievement of goals that brings satisfaction but the act of *seeking* itself. According to Jaak Panksepp in his book *Affective Neuroscience*, seeking is one of the human brain's core instincts. Every mammal has the natural urge to explore their surroundings and seek new food sources and habitats. This explains why achieving a goal doesn't bring long-term happiness.

The continual act of looking ahead, forming new desires, and actively pursuing them results in a lifetime of satisfaction and happiness. Essentially, your wish list for your life will never be complete, and it shouldn't.

When you stop wanting, expanding, and seeking, you stop *living*.

Now that you understand that wanting more is natural, let's clarify what will provide the satisfaction and fulfillment you seek. You must get off the proverbial hamster wheel of thinking "I'll be happy when . . ."

THE HAMSTER WHEEL

One of my friends, Michael, had just gotten a new job. He was filled with energy and excitement as each day brought the opportunity to meet new people, learn new skills, challenge his abilities, and try new things. He felt so grateful for this opportunity and believed he had found a company he could grow within for years to come.

A year later, Michael's initial excitement turned into apathy and boredom. He was still in the same job, working with the same people, providing the same functions. However, he no longer found joy in what he was doing. His motivation dropped considerably, and he started dreading Monday mornings. He no longer perceived his job with excitement and gratitude; it now felt like *work*.

When I asked him what had changed, he blamed his boss for being too demanding, his colleagues for being lazy, and the company for not paying him what he was worth. He shared that he had already started looking for a new job because this one wouldn't work out. I recommended that he take some time to think about what he wanted and why he felt unsatisfied and unfulfilled *before* leaving his job for another.

He didn't take my advice.

Michael did find a new job with a better job title and a higher paycheck. He was jazzed and felt excited about this new opportunity. Michael believed he had *finally* found the perfect job for him—this was the job he wouldn't want to leave. Eighteen months later, he called to tell me he was unsatisfied and unfulfilled with his current situation and needed to look for a different job again.

You'll get the same results if you continue doing the same things. You job-hop enough times and you'll start to believe that maybe you're not meant to feel fulfilled at work.

The antidote to a life on the hamster wheel is to shift into living your *purpose*. Before we clarify what is your purpose and what is not, I have to share something with you.

You are a living *genius*.

Every human being is born a genius. Hear me out. The word "genus" means a rank of classification of organisms. Humans are all a part of the genus, Homo (the scientific name for our species is Homo sapiens).

So, if we're part of the same genus, what makes you a genius? The only difference between the words "genus" and "genius" is the letter "I," which refers to a human's unique spirit, innate ability, and superior talent. The "I" separates you from everyone else in the human species, expressed through your unique perspective, creativity, originality, and skill.

When you connect to and express your genius in the world, you are living at your Zenith—achieving your highest potential for your lifetime. This is the version of you shining so bright others can't help but see and want to be near you.

When you're tapped into and sharing your inner genius, you become a joyful, inspiring, positive, magnetic human to be around. You feel like you're swimming along a current that is propelling you forward in magical ways.

So, how does being a genius relate to your purpose?

Because your purpose *is* to share your unique genius with the world, and when you do, you get the reward of living a life filled with meaning, love, joy, impact, and more abundance than you could ever imagine.

This is your calling.

I love this quote from Oprah Winfrey: "There is no greater gift you can give or receive than to honor your calling. It's why you were born. And how you become most truly alive."

Considering how essential purpose is to our overall life experience, it's amazing how much confusion there is around the true meaning of that word.

WHAT IS PURPOSE?

According to the Oxford English Dictionary, purpose is: "the reason for which something is done or created or for which something exists."

The nature of purpose is intangible; you can't grab it with both hands and say, "Here it is! I've found it!" This is why it can feel illusory and out of reach. We can't see it, touch it, hear it, taste it—but we can *feel* it.

Your purpose is the primary motivating aim of your life, or simply, it's the reason you get up in the morning. Your purpose will help guide your life decisions, influence your behavior, shape your goals, offer a sense of direction, and create meaning in your life. Your purpose isn't just what you do, it's also the *spirit* with which you do it.

In my experience hosting corporate trainings on this topic, it's often easier to grasp what purpose is by understanding what it is *not.*

What follows are some common myths about purpose.

Myth #1. You need to find your purpose.

Have you ever lost your keys in your house and spent hours frantically searching in every drawer, handbag, and room, only to find that they've been in your pocket all along?

You've never *lost* your purpose because you can't lose something that's a part of you.

When you believe your purpose is something you must find, it leads you on a wild goose chase, running after something outside yourself. You don't need to find your purpose—you need to *align* with your purpose. This journey is an inside-out approach and requires you to focus inward to acquire a deep knowledge of yourself.

I believe the reason many people struggle to gain self-confidence, self-worth, and self-esteem is that they haven't embraced their inner genius.

Think about it: How would you show up if you knew you had this valuable superpower inside you? Would you feel more confident in your abilities and more worthy of being seen and heard? How would this knowledge affect your self-image?

When you stop trying to find your purpose, you will realize it was always there, just waiting for you to claim it.

Myth #2. Your purpose is within a specific job or job title.

Your purpose is not a job title. I wasn't born to be the senior vice president of the company I work for. If my job title were my purpose, what would happen if I left my job? Would I be *purposeless*?

My current job is the *vehicle* through which I'm expressing my purpose. However, I can express my purpose in many jobs, titles, and situations.

It's important to note that you can express your purpose in ways that aren't connected to a job or a paycheck. For instance, I met a woman who felt called to serve the homeless community and spent hours after work and on weekends volunteering at local shelters. One of my colleagues is passionate about connecting rescue dogs with good homes, so she regularly fosters orphaned puppies, ensuring they receive love and support until they are placed with a family.

Your purpose is an ever-moving target. As you change, how you express your purpose will evolve too. It's more about knowing you have unique inner gifts and talents you should express and then looking for opportunities in your everyday life to share them.

The details of where you work do not define your purpose. But you must bring your purpose *with you* wherever you work.

Myth #3. Someone else can tell you your purpose.

You are the foremost expert on you. No one else can tell you what your purpose is in this lifetime. You'll recognize your purpose by how it feels on the *inside,* which means no one else can identify it for you—not your mom, not your best friend, not your husband or wife, not your children, not a spiritual guru, not a psychic, and not the nice woman sitting next to you on the bus.

I believe there's an aspect of you—your higher self or your soul—that is deeply aware of what you are meant to do in this lifetime. That brilliant, all-knowing part of you is ready and willing to share that information—but it is only by looking within that you will find the clarity you seek.

YOUR PURPOSE IS A STATE OF BEING

In my experience, purpose is more about who you are *being* than what you are doing.

At one point in my professional career, I lived two different lives.

By day, I was a high-level executive driving sales teams and handling clients. After hours, I was a coach and spiritual mentor, hosting group coaching events and writing inspirational content before the sun came up every morning.

I knew without a shadow of a doubt what my purpose was, but I believed it had nothing to do with my current job title or function. I didn't feel safe or comfortable enough to share what I was doing outside of work with my colleagues. I certainly didn't think bringing my passion for personal development and spirituality into the workplace would be acceptable. In my mind, it was better to keep the two parts of my life separate. I didn't want my colleagues to think I was crazy, and I didn't want to lose their respect—or, even worse, my job.

I believed that to live and express my purpose fully, I would have to get the hell out of Corporate America. I felt profoundly unfulfilled and unsatisfied, and I projected *all* that negative emotion onto the job I was in—because I believed it was the job's fault that I felt this way.

As fortune would have it, Rudi was offered a high-level job at the company I was working for, and he accepted. I was worried that Rudi would hate it, knowing that he wasn't used to editing his thoughts and would need to filter down some of the "spiritual talk" around the office. Turns out, Rudi had no intention of filtering anything. He responded to my advice, "I'm showing up as me, and if they don't like it, I'll leave."

And that's what he did. He didn't show up as the executive responsible for driving the sales teams; he showed up as Rudi, the transformational, high-performance coach. He was motivating, inspiring, and intense, and he spent more time coaching individuals than he did hosting sales calls and strategy meetings.

I watched in awe as the company's sales revenue climbed to unbelievable heights, and the teams started showing up with more personal accountability, integrity, and excitement for their jobs. To my surprise, no one was laughing at him for saying things like "I love you" at the end of a meeting, nor threatening to fire him for his unconventional approach to sales.

Rudi was being *Rudi*, sharing his unique genius, expressing his purpose unapologetically—and it was creating miracles.

This was the wake-up call I needed. I knew my purpose was to inspire and uplift people, but I thought it had to come in the form of a coaching program or someone reading my book. It never occurred to me that I could express my purpose in my current job.

The problem hadn't been my job—it had been *me.*

I had been waiting for the perfect time and place to start sharing my gifts openly instead of starting right where I was, trusting I was there for a reason. This was a missed opportunity, and I wouldn't let it happen again.

Fast-forward a few years, and an opportunity fell in my lap to apply for a high-level position at a growing company in the same industry. During the interview, in addition to sharing my prior work experience, I shared my passion for personal development, coaching, and training. I expressed my desire to share that gift with the organization in addition to fulfilling my job function. The company's president smiled and said, "I want you to bring *all* of you to this job. We want it all."

And that's what I did. My first day on the job was spent hosting a virtual training for over three hundred employees, teaching them how to identify and release their limiting beliefs. I have since hosted many more mindset and personal development trainings for the company and continue to do so.

For the first time in my life, I showed up as my authentic self at work and sought opportunities to share my gifts, coaching, and insights with my colleagues. I have never felt more seen, valued, appreciated, and fulfilled as I have working for this organization. And while this company and the people in it are simply extraordinary, I know that my experience directly reflects how *I* have chosen to show up.

I know now that I get to *be* my purpose wherever I go, which means I get to be happy and fulfilled no matter what.

HOW TO ALIGN WITH YOUR PURPOSE

Remember, you are not *finding* your purpose, you are *aligning* with it. What follows are the steps you can take to clarify what your purpose is and how you can make the minor (and sometimes major) adjustments needed to align with the life you were born to live.

Identify your passions

I love this quote from bestselling author and pastor Bishop T.D. Jakes: "If you can't figure out your purpose, figure out your passion. For your passion will lead you right into your purpose."

When you share your passion with others, it becomes your purpose.

In my experience, the passions that I have carried the longest are the ones that have played the most prominent part in my purpose. I loved books and writing from an early age, was obsessed with international travel, loved listening and offering advice to friends and family when they were having problems, and became passionate about learning everything I could about personal development, neuroscience, and spirituality.

Your passions become signposts on your journey, pointing you in the direction of your purpose.

So, what are yours?

Consider the following questions:

- What is something you loved to do when you were younger?
- What is something you are good at doing?

- What is something that makes you forget about the time, eating, going to bed, or any of your responsibilities when you're in the flow of doing it?
- What is something you can talk about for hours—that lights you up, gets you excited, and gives you energy when you talk about it?
- What is something you regularly look forward to doing?
- What is something you love learning about?
- What is something you spend your extra money on?

It's common to lose touch with your natural inborn passions, especially if your culture doesn't accept or celebrate what you're passionate about. There are *no* silly, trivial, or useless passions.

Turn your passion into purpose

- Doing something you love = passion
- Doing something you love and that serves others = purpose

Your gifts are not yours to hide and hoard—they are meant to be opened and shared with others. And in the process of sharing your unique superpowers, you will be rewarded with the sweetness of fulfillment and joy.

What if you woke up tomorrow and money no longer existed? You now had to barter services to ensure you and your family were provided for. You didn't have time to master a new craft or learn something new. You had to pull from your natural gifts, passions, and interests.

What would you offer?

Would you teach young children to read? Would you create music for others to listen to? Would you paint pictures of people's animals? Would you offer group fitness classes? Would you provide first aid care for injuries?

Interestingly, this scenario plays out in real life when tragedy strikes a community or country. The people rock up, ready to help in any way *they can.* Studies have shown that people who jumped in to help and volunteer reported heightened feelings of fulfillment for weeks and even months after the event. When we share our gifts, we feel happier.

How can you start sharing your passions in your current situation? In what ways could others need the gifts you have to share? And how can you positively impact their lives—physically, mentally, and emotionally?

Assign meaning to the present

One of my favorite quotes of all time is by Holocaust survivor and author of *Man's Search for Meaning*, Viktor E. Frankl: "Life is never made unbearable by circumstances, but only by lack of meaning and purpose."

So, how do you find meaning in your present? How do you find purpose in the darkest, most challenging situations?

There is a reason you are where you are. It could be to learn an important skill, overcome a fear, master a gift, learn how to communicate, or provide money while you're building a business or opportunity that's more fulfilling.

I want to share a powerful metaphor that illustrates this idea.

Imagine you've just started playing a video game with hundreds of levels. Each level presents different challenges you must move through, each one an opportunity to master skills that will be necessary for clearing future levels.

As you progress from level to level, the experience you gain from earlier challenges will come in handy, and you'll be better equipped to handle whatever obstacles come your way. The journey will still be challenging, but you'll have an arsenal of skills at your disposal.

You'll occasionally get stuck on a level, experiencing many failed attempts, until that one time when you'll finally be able to do what you couldn't before, and you'll complete the level. If you were to try and skip levels, you likely wouldn't be successful because you'd lack the skills you would have learned in the levels you missed.

While trivial, the video game is an excellent metaphor for life and how your purpose can show up at any moment. There's no point in trying to forecast your purpose in ten years. The point is to trust that you're exactly where you need to be and to assign meaning to what you're doing now, knowing that it's serving and preparing you for what's to come.

You are constantly being *qualified* to fulfill your purpose. Every experience is preparing you for the next. Trust that you're where you must be, and keep your eyes and heart open for the breadcrumbs leading you forward.

Prioritize your purpose

Let's pretend you woke up to find $86,400 deposited in your checking account, and it was legally yours with one stipulation: you had to spend it within twenty-four hours. Otherwise, it would disappear from your account. How would you spend it? Would you hit snooze and sleep in till noon, binge-watch a Netflix series, and get lost for hours scrolling through Instagram?

Or would you jump out of bed, excited about how you could change your life with the money you were gifted? Would you research ways to invest so you could grow that money? Would you figure out ways to support your family and friends? Would you spend it in ways that would help you fulfill your greatest dreams and desires?

We all wake up with the same amount of time in a day: 86,400 seconds. How we spend that time separates us and creates the overall quality of our lives.

How much time are you spending honing your skills and becoming a master of your craft? Just because you're naturally good at something doesn't mean you don't have to work at it. You are responsible for nurturing and growing that gift, sharing it, and positively impacting others.

The hours of 4:30 a.m. to 6:30 a.m. are my magic hours. Those are the hours I dedicate to creating content that will impact the world. I carve out those two precious hours in my day to ensure my purpose receives top priority. And the reward is starting every day feeling energized, creatively inspired, and unbelievably fulfilled. Do the things that bring you joy, and you will live a joyful life—it's that simple, folks.

How can you prioritize your purpose?

- Wake up earlier and dedicate time to doing what you *love.*
- Create time to get quiet and receive inspiration. Meditation is an excellent tool for this!
- Actively seek out opportunities to do what lights you up.
- Show and tell others what your unique genius is. You never know who might need what you have to give!

Create your purpose commitment

Many years ago, as part of a transformational leadership course, I was asked to create my purpose commitment—a one-sentence declaration of who *I am* and what I'm here to *do*.

I had never consolidated my life's purpose into one sentence; honestly, the task felt daunting. How could I encapsulate what I think I'm meant to be and do in so few words?

Here's what I found: having that level of clarity is not only possible but extremely powerful. I took my time writing out version after version until I landed on one that felt right. I then printed it out, signed it, and hung it up in my office so I would see it daily. This singular sentence has become my North Star. It's a reminder that my life matters, my gifts are important, and it's my responsibility to use them to serve others.

What follows is my purpose commitment:

I am a powerful, authentic, inspiring leader who uses my words to open hearts and remind individuals of their worth, power, and unlimited nature.

As author and motivational speaker Leo Buscaglia wrote, "It's not enough to have lived. We should be determined to live for something."

It's time for you to define your purpose.

PUTTING IT INTO PRACTICE

A purpose commitment defines who you are and the mark you want to leave on this world. It provides clarity and reflects commitment to your goals. This statement anchors you in the direction you want your story to go. It serves as a guiding principle as you consider opportunities, enabling you to question: "Will this support me in aligning with my purpose?"

Consider the following suggestions as you compose your purpose commitment.

- **Brainstorm:** Allow time for quiet reflection to think about the following questions:

  How do I want to make a *difference* in the world?

  How do I want to be *remembered*?

  What kind of *legacy* do I want to leave behind?

- **Compose your first draft:** Use your answers to these questions to guide your writing:

  Who am I?

  What qualities do I possess? (e.g., courageous, inspiring, loving)

  What do I do?

  Who do I do it for?

  How does my work serve the wants or needs of others?

  How are other people changed by my actions?

Permit yourself to write a draft of your purpose commitment without making corrections. Don't overanalyze it. Overthinking can paralyze you in this process. Write *something*. Edit later.

- **Choose words that reflect positive action:** Instead of stating what you want to avoid, choose positive words that reflect what you want to be, do, and experience.

- **Write in present tense:** Your purpose commitment reflects who you are and what you bring to the world—beginning today. Focus your intention on what you envision for your life. Describe the personal mark you want to make on this planet. State it in present tense: "I am," "I do," but refrain from using "I will."

- **Revise your commitment:** Your purpose commitment is a work in progress. Sometimes words flow more easily after stepping away from the page for a bit. As you make time to edit your personal purpose statement, you will find words that reflect what you want to express.

- **Sign it:** Allow space for your signature at the bottom of the page. A signature reflects a commitment to your words. As a result, you will make choices that align with your purpose commitment and, consequently, your goals.

- **Display it:** Frame or display your personal purpose commitment in a place where you will see it often. The daily reminder of seeing, reading, reflecting upon, and internalizing your personal purpose commitment becomes a directional compass that will guide your words, actions, decisions, and behaviors.

What follows are a few examples of powerful purpose commitments: Feel free to add yours to the list!

- I serve others as a leader, live a balanced life, and apply ethical principles to make a significant difference in the world.
- My purpose is to be a beacon of light, a bridge of understanding, a

tower of integrity, and an inspiration to others as a speaker, writer, and entrepreneur.

- I am a loving, compassionate, creative teacher who spreads love and positivity through art and music.
- I am a courageous, abundant, passionate creator here to bring new ideas and innovations into the world that will positively impact people's lives.

Chapter 4

MANIFEST YOUR NEW VISION

When you want something, all the universe
conspires in helping you to achieve it.
—Paulo Coelho, *The Alchemist*

NOW THAT YOU KNOW *WHAT* you want, your deepest desires for your life, how will you make them a reality?

I believe your desires want *you* as much as you want them. But there are better strategies than sitting on your couch expecting them to appear on your doorstep. You will need every tool at your disposal, and one of the most powerful is your ability to manifest.

Your unique desires are gifts from your *soul,* and they are beautifully connected to your purpose. They deserve to be acknowledged, honored, and intentionally created as the gifts they are.

My son, Brady, has shared a dream of becoming a professional singer since he could talk. When we sit down to watch *The Voice* as a family, he'll look at us with tears in his eyes and say, "I don't know why I'm crying; I just have this feeling *I will do this one day.*"

Brady didn't inherit the dream to be a singer from Rudi and me. We didn't tell him this was his heart's desire. He was born with it already within him, placed there for him to find, acknowledge, and create.

It's common to assume your dreams are the creations of an overactive imagination. We have been taught that our imagination is not to be trusted—a faulty function of the logical mind that doesn't show us what is realistic and possible. This couldn't be further from the truth. Your imagination is an unbelievable tool.

Some of the most accomplished individuals in history have shared this truth during a time when the world wasn't primed and open to hearing it. Self-help guru and author of *Think and Grow Rich,* Napoleon Hill was born in 1883; in the early 1900s, he taught, "If you can conceive it, you can achieve it." American animator and film producer Walt Disney believed, "If you can dream it, you can do it." And one of my favorite quotes, often attributed to Albert Einstein, is "Imagination is everything. It is the preview of life's coming attractions."

Your unique inner desires are there for you to create and experience—and doing so is your responsibility. They are there to lead you to a specific destination, which will then lead to the next desire and goal. Remember, your purpose is in a constant state of unfolding.

So, how do you ensure you don't die with your biggest, most significant dreams unfulfilled?

You need to acknowledge and master your ability to create your reality.

MANIFESTATION 101

The word "manifestation" has become mainstream in the last few decades. Yet, plenty of people still think it's complete bullshit.

If you search the word "manifestation" on Wikipedia, you'll see that it's defined as "the act of becoming manifest, to become perceptible to the senses." To put it simply, to manifest is to hold an intention for something and remain conscious of it happening in real life; to take a thought and make it matter.

Manifesting has primarily been delegated to the "woo-woo" spiritual category because it's in the weird gray area that science hasn't fully explained, at least until recently. We're in an exciting time when science is beginning to intersect with the spiritual in fascinating ways.

For instance, quantum physicists suggest that our thoughts and emotions directly influence the energy that makes up our reality. While there are still a lot of *unknowns* about how our energy impacts reality, it is becoming more apparent that the thoughts we think and emotions we feel catalyze a mysterious reaction in the quantum field of pure potential; the effect is seen in our external reality.

This also indicates that our external world is not the cause of our inner emotions. It's the other way around. Our inner world has a profound effect on our external world. To put it simply, your outer reality is a mirror of what is happening within you.

You could spend a lifetime debating the existence or nonexistence of your ability to manifest, whether it is fact or fiction, and you'll find evidence to validate both sides. Or, you can look back at your own life experience to find the proof you seek.

Have you ever experienced receiving something you desired in a way that appeared coincidental and synchronistic? Alternatively, have you experienced receiving something you were fearing and stressing about?

I learned about manifestation in my early twenties and have collected hundreds of examples of how I have consciously and intentionally manifested things. My confidence in my ability to manifest is sky-high because I've found too much proof to doubt it any longer.

Rudi and I approach manifestation as a game and have created some of the most unbelievable things and experiences this way. We've consciously manifested hotel room upgrades, first-class flights, unexpected checks in the mail, money to fund home renovations, job promotions, new clients, free press, podcast guests, grand prizes in contests, physical healing for chronic pain, free furniture, book editors, unexpected refunds that came just when we needed the money, free vacations, and even *each other*.

When I say *consciously* manifest, I mean that we are fully aware of our abilities to co-create our reality with the Universe and intentionally call things, people, and experiences into our lives.

Look around at everything in your space right now—clothing, furniture, kitchen utensils, desk, even the home, office, or park bench you sit in now. It was once just an invisible, intangible idea that someone decided to apply their focus and energy to create in physical form.

You are manifesting whether you are aware of it or not. Just by entertaining a thought in your mind right now, which elicits an emotional response, you are affecting your reality.

Don't you want to figure out how to master and maximize this inborn superpower for your benefit?

BECOME A MASTER MANIFESTER

When you genuinely believe that you have the power to create your reality, life gets really interesting. Suddenly, that big dream or desire you've carried doesn't feel so impossibly out of reach. Like any other skill you've mastered, the more you practice consciously manifesting, the more confident and proficient you will become at it.

I will take you through the process I follow and teach you to manifest your reality consciously. I don't believe there's *one* way to do anything, but the following strategy is a great jumping-off point until you find what feels right for you.

#1. Declare what you want and why you want it

Make a list of the dreams and desires that are most important to you. Next to each one, write out *why* you want that. And then ask yourself how the achievement of what you seek will make you feel.

For instance, if you sincerely desire a job promotion, think about why you want that. Is it because of the increase in pay, power, and influence, or maybe recognition? Write down what the reason is for you. Then, identify how you believe you will feel when you receive this promotion. Is it joy? Security? Pride?

It will help if you get clear on the *what* and the *why*, because underneath every desire is a belief that it will make you feel a certain way. If you can understand what you want to feel, you might find a way to start feeling that way *now.*

After you've made your list, choose one or two goals to focus on. It will be tempting to try and manifest everything at once, but that strategy isn't very effective. Your focus is extremely powerful—what you focus on expands, but if you focus on too many things at once, you will weaken your manifestation power.

If you stood at the edge of a pond and threw a handful of tiny rocks into the water, it would create many small ripples that would quickly dissipate. But if you instead dropped a giant boulder into the water, the wave created would be much bigger and would affect the whole pond. Your most important dreams deserve to be the giant boulder, which will require consistent focus, commitment, and determination.

I also recommend that you keep your list private. Your heart's desires deserve to be protected, just as you would treat a fragile hatchling. For instance, don't call your mom and tell her *everything* you are creating unless you are confident she will be supportive and encouraging. Here's why: Many great dreams have been squashed by well-meaning parents, family, and friends who project their fears and disbelief onto one's life experience. It's much better to surprise them all when you *show* them what you've created! Eventually, they'll get on board.

#2. Align your thoughts and emotions

To manifest, you need to think *and* feel. Imagine each of your thoughts as a rocket of desire and the corresponding emotion or feeling as a magnet drawing the experience back to you.

Thought alone isn't enough; you must have the aligned feeling to draw it back to you. You don't attract what you think about so much as what you *feel.* This is the part of the manifestation process that individuals get all wrong. They spend a lot of time thinking about what they want, but they don't do the work to curate and align their emotions to match what they want to manifest.

For instance, let's say you want to manifest more abundance in your life. You visualize yourself enjoying the freedom of having plenty of money to pay your bills and take exciting vacations—but you don't *feel* abundant.

The thought and emotion aren't aligned; thus, the manifestation link is broken. You'll more likely continue to create lack; while your conscious thoughts are of more money, your *subconscious* belief system (causing the feeling of lack) is running the "I'll never have enough money" program . . . and you're probably not even aware of it.

In Part 2 of this book, you'll find an entire chapter dedicated to helping you address existing limiting beliefs. I explain how you got these beliefs and the steps you can take to create a belief system that will support your dreams instead of hinder them.

The main culprit for manifestations not coming to pass is a subconscious belief that you are not *worthy* of having what you desire. Renowned motivational speaker Les Brown put it best when he said, "Whatever you accomplish in life is a manifestation not as much of what you do, as of what you believe you deserve."

If you're looking to your past self as an indicator of who you will be in the future, you will continue to create the same circumstances. But if you're courageous and willing to work on up-leveling your belief system, the world will open up to you in miraculous ways. Remember, your external reality is a mirror; it's just feedback for what's going on within you.

In addition to addressing your subconscious belief system, you'll also need to intentionally synchronize your energy with the frequency of your desire.

#3. Cultivate a positive emotional state

Your energy needs to match the frequency of what you desire. The best way to do this is to cultivate heightened emotion intentionally.

Shit is going to happen. You'll have crappy days and go through challenging periods in your life. Negative emotions aren't wrong—in fact, no emotion is inherently destructive. It's when you start to identify *as* these emotions that they become problematic (e.g., I *am* depressed, I *am* anxious).

Living in a chronic emotional state of depression, anxiety, stress, and fear can negatively impact your ability to manifest.

If you're waiting for something to happen outside of you to feel better, you will be waiting a long time.

Special effects artist and channeler Darryl Anka said, "Everything is energy, and that is all there is to it. Match the frequency of the reality you want, and you cannot help but get that reality. It can be no other way. This is not philosophy. This is physics."

My advice is to take accountability for your emotional state and spend time every day cultivating positive emotions. The benefit to this is you will not only feel better but will also put yourself into a position to match the frequency of what you desire.

So, how do you match your energetic frequency to your desired frequency? I recommend you incorporate a practice of cultivating heightened emotion in your daily morning routine.

Let me give you a quick example of how you can do this.

I want you to close your eyes and picture someone you love unconditionally—a spouse, child, or pet. Hold the picture in your mind until you start to feel your heart open and a warm feeling of love, adoration, and gratitude spread through you. Imagine giving that person or animal a hug and a kiss, thanking them for being a part of your life. Focus on the heightened emotion and allow it to spread throughout your body until you feel like it's pouring out of you.

Congratulations, you self-generated the most coveted feelings of love and gratitude. You didn't rely on something outside of you to make you feel that way—you cultivated positive emotion on your own. If you can generate love and gratitude within, you can also create feelings of abundance, freedom, power, and joy.

Now, go back to the first step in the manifestation process. What emotion do you believe you will feel when you achieve the desires on your list?

Is it freedom? If so, you need to feel and emote the energetic frequency of freedom to become a match to it.

How else can you feel the emotion of freedom? Actively look to do the things that make you feel free. Take a walk during your lunch break; take that vacation you've been dreaming about; block off your calendar on a Friday afternoon to do something you love. The more you curate opportunities to feel *free,* the more you embody the energy of freedom. And you'll be well on your way to manifesting more of it.

> DON'T EVER FORGET THIS: YOU DON'T MANIFEST WHAT YOU WANT; YOU MANIFEST WHAT YOU *ARE.* START BEING THE PERSON YOU WANT TO BE.

#4. Take action

While we all secretly pine for the genie in a bottle that will instantly grant whatever we wish, manifestation, unfortunately, requires you to *do* something. In my experience, taking action on a desire before it's made manifest kicks the forward momentum into high gear.

Taking an action, regardless of the size, is the energetic equivalent of a quantum leap forward. It'll also give you the feeling of positive progress, which is vital to staying committed and focused on your goal.

According to American naturalist, essayist, poet, and philosopher Henry David Thoreau, "If one advances confidently in the direction of his dreams, and endeavors to live the life which he has imagined, he will meet with a success unexpected in common hours."

Make a list of what you must do to reach your goal and commit to fulfilling one action daily. Before you know it, when you least expect it, you will meet your desire.

#5. Act as if you already have what you desire

One of my greatest spiritual teachers and mentors has been Dr. Wayne Dyer. He taught that to create the life of your dreams, you must practice living from the end. Before beginning to write a book, he would design the cover and wrap an existing book with it. This symbol sitting on his writing desk would remind him that the book is already finished, published, and is a *New York Times* bestseller.

He took this practice to everything in his life, and lo and behold, he achieved a hell of a lot and helped millions of people!

Why wait until you receive your manifestation to celebrate and feel good?

I'm a big fan of creating a visualization practice. What if you woke up every morning and imagined a scene in your mind's eye of having achieved the desire you seek? Insert yourself into the scene as if you're experiencing it now.

In addition to helping you cultivate a heightened emotion, visualization enables you to reach your goals because it prepares your mind and body ahead of time. Your subconscious doesn't know the difference between what is in your imagination and what isn't. The more you visualize experiencing something, the easier it will be to shift your belief system and feel that something is possible.

I know this process seems *way* too simple. But it's often the most straightforward action that can create the most significant results.

#6. Let go and surrender

The sixth and final step is one of the most important.

Your manifestation will rarely come in the way you think it will. Why? Because your mind is limited in its ability to imagine potential outcomes, while the Universe is *unlimited.*

There are an infinite number of ways in which your desire could manifest, and holding tightly to one way because it's the only way you can think of will cause resistance to receiving what you seek. It's also possible that what you want will show up, but because it doesn't look how you expected it to look, you won't recognize it as the gift it was intended to be.

The Universe will not only bring you what you desire, but it will also come with the feeling you desire and do so in a way that will serve the highest good of everyone involved. Remember, we are all connected, and one manifestation can serve the needs of so many.

This will require you to build trust because no amount of forcing and flexing your muscles will bring you your desire any sooner. It will come in the perfect way, right on time.

You must relax, loosen your grip, and allow the all-powerful, all-knowing Universe to work its magic.

PUTTING IT INTO PRACTICE

Start with the small stuff. I recommend you start building your belief that you can successfully manifest by selecting something on your list that *isn't* that important to you. This is because it's often the big desires that you unconsciously create resistance to manifesting. After all, the stakes are high, and you fear failure.

Look at your list and pick something small, such as finding a specific piece of clothing or manifesting $100. Treat this as an experiment and take your desire through the following steps.

- Identify why you want this and how you will feel when you get it.
- Investigate whether you have limiting beliefs about your ability and worthiness to receive your desire.
- Identify one or two actions you can start taking every day to get this manifestation moving.
- Every morning and evening, spend time visualizing this item or

experience as if you already have it. Make it as vivid as possible and *feel* the positive emotions.

- Avoid letting your mind try to predict how this will happen, and stay open to what comes your way.

Part 2

PREPARE FOR THE OBSTACLES

Chapter 5

MANAGE YOUR FEARS

The brave man is not he who does not feel
afraid, but he who conquers that fear.

—Nelson Mandela

IN 2008, I WENT ON a trip with my best friend Holli to Maui. We were both in our twenties and single, so we thought a fun getaway to a beautiful beach to drink copious amounts of cocktails and meet cute boys was a great idea. Upon getting there, we soon found out that Maui was the ultimate honeymoon and anniversary destination, so rather than lie on the beach among all the newlyweds, we shifted gears and set our sights on adventure. We took surf lessons, flew in a helicopter, went snorkeling, and took long drives around the island, going down winding roads, stopping to take pictures of the beautiful scenery and hidden waterfalls.

On one of our many stops, we noticed people were hiking up to the top of the waterfall and jumping off one of the ledges into the plunge pool below. Nothing about this seemed like a good idea; however, Holli grabbed my hand and said, "Let's go!"

I nervously followed her while watching tourists take the leap and resurface with big smiles on their faces. We got in line, and when it was her turn, she looked back and yelled, "See you on the other side!" and then gracefully jumped off the ledge without a care in the world. I peered over to ensure she was okay and felt relief when I saw her smiling back at me.

It was my turn. I took a few deep breaths, preparing myself to jump. Then, something happened. It was as if I lost all feeling in my legs, and my whole body began to shake. My heart started beating fast. I was immobilized. Holli was yelling, "Jump!" from below, and a group of bystanders joined in the cheering. The line behind me grew restless, so I stepped aside and let the people behind me go ahead.

I stood on that ledge for almost an *hour*, an excruciating sixty minutes of considering whether to jump or head back down. Whenever I gathered the courage to reapproach the ledge, the same fear would take over my body. Eventually, an older man in line who had no doubt witnessed my full-on panic attack approached and said, "Excuse me, ma'am, can I give you some advice? It would help if you made a decision. Are you going to jump or not? Once you decide, don't give yourself time to think about it—just do it."

This stranger delivered a significant truth bomb, precisely what I needed to hear. I realized I hadn't decided, so my mind was choosing for me, and my body was following its command. I silently asked myself: *How will I feel if I don't take this leap?* Answer: disappointed and weak. I then asked myself: *How will I feel if I do?* Answer: damn proud of myself.

At this point, about fifty people below were cheering me on (*so humiliating*). I took a deep breath and said, "To hell with it." I took off running toward that ledge like my life depended on it and screamed all the way down. I felt relief, joy, and pride as my body plunged into the cool, crisp water below. I had overcome my fear in that moment, and I felt invincible.

I leaped over that beautiful waterfall five more times that day.

While this experience seems inconsequential, it profoundly affected how I live my life. I have been on that proverbial ledge more times than I can count. It generally starts with an inspired idea or a big dream I long to achieve. I begin by imagining how awesome it will be to have, be, or do this thing; once I reach the ledge of no return, that point where I have to put some skin in the game, I pause long enough for doubt and fear to set in. The idea that seemed so expansive and exciting now feels impossible, and I consider giving it up to avoid the possible pain on the other side. But then I ask myself that same question: *How will I feel if I don't reach this goal? And how will I feel if I do?* More often than not, I leap.

On the other side of fear is *freedom*. Deciding to jump despite the anxiety I was experiencing allowed me to see the fear for what it was—an illusion. As American industrialist and business magnate Henry Ford so brilliantly said, "One of the greatest discoveries a man makes, one of his great surprises, is to find he can do what he was afraid he couldn't do."

Sometimes, the proverbial ledge represents a job change, ending a relationship, having a difficult conversation, or moving to another state. But it can also (and often does) mean sharing your gifts with the world—taking the actions necessary to fulfill your purpose.

If you want to change anything in your life, you have to grow and change. Your growth will require you to push past the edges of your comfort zone, triggering your built-in security system, a.k.a. your fears.

To *show up authentically*, you have to face your fears.

To *share your gifts with the world*, you have to face your fears.

To *take the necessary risks*, you have to face your fears.

To *grow beyond the person you've been until now*, you have to face your fears.

The good news is you can develop the skill of fear management and transformation. And *that* is a skill worth its weight in gold.

WHAT IS FEAR?

There are two types of fear—innate and learned. Innate fears are hardwired in the human brain and are beneficial as they keep us safe. A few examples of innate fears are death, loud noises, and falling. The innate fear response comes encoded in the brain, meaning it doesn't require prior experience.

Alternatively, learned fears are typically developed at a young age and are influenced by your environment, experiences, and social learning.

Some fear is *good*; it can warn you of impending danger and keep you from leaning too far over the ledge or getting hit by an oncoming car. But what about self-created fears that flare up when you're not in danger? These fears live in your imagination and are focused on a future experience that doesn't exist yet. Self-created fear can be described with the following acronym.

F.E.A.R: False Evidence Appearing Real

Fear is an illusion, even though it might feel incredibly real, so much so that you act *as though* it were real. You must become aware of these destructive, self-created fears running unconsciously behind the scenes in your mind and body.

THE BIG SEVEN

Just as Africa's Big Five refers to the most dangerous animals that are the hardest to catch and kill, I'd like to introduce you to seven of the most common underlying fears that are equally sneaky and have the potential to immobilize you or make you sprint in the opposite direction of your intended goal.

#1. Fear of abandonment

This is the fear that the people close to you will leave, and it often is born from an experience in childhood that you perceived as abandonment. For instance, if you experienced great pain and sadness when your parents left you in daycare as a toddler, your brain could have processed that negative experience as abandonment and now wants to protect you from ever feeling that way again. Fast forward to your twenties, and you can't understand why you keep a wall up, not letting anyone fully in. Thus, you're unable to maintain a long-term relationship, constantly pushing people away before they can leave you.

#2. Fear of failure

This fear can look like avoiding any activity, scenario, or experience that has the potential for an unsuccessful outcome. Fear of failure is often caused by overly critical parents or heightened negative emotions when you failed at something when you were young. For instance, if you did poorly while delivering a presentation in school and felt humiliated, you could carry that forward and avoid public speaking altogether. Symptoms of fear of failure can be procrastination, self-sabotage, low self-esteem, and perfectionism.

#3. Fear of success

This fear is rooted in the belief that if you achieve your goal, you won't be good enough or capable enough to sustain success. Interestingly, fear of success can come from the experience of others feeling bad when you achieved something and they didn't. It can also come from carrying the guilt of doing better than others, which causes you to diminish yourself and your abilities in order to make others feel better. The symptoms of this can include setting low goals, only choosing those dreams and desires you feel comfortable with, or perfectionism, which means you set your expectations so high that you never complete your intended goal and succeed.

#4. Fear of rejection

People who are afraid of being rejected, criticized, and humiliated desperately want to be liked and accepted at all costs and avoid doing anything that may result in being disliked, which makes it virtually impossible to show up authentically. This fear often comes from experiencing the loss of a parent or loved one early in life, divorce, bullying, or being made to believe you're not accepted or are somehow different from your peers. The common symptoms include preoccupation with what others think of you, low self-esteem, shame, anxiety, and indecisiveness. Codependency is also a common symptom, which can look like people-pleasing, becoming what others want you to be, and needing everyone else to be okay at the cost of your own comfort and well-being.

#5. Fear of loss

This fear can be particularly debilitating. It's the fear of experiencing the intense pain associated with losing someone. It can lead to extreme thoughts of death and fear of situations that might lead to death, including phobias. When someone suffers from this fear, they are overprotective of their loved ones and worry nonstop about their health and safety. It's rooted in a great fear of the unknown and a deep desire to control all outcomes in life.

#6. Fear of judgment

Fear of judgment, often associated with social anxiety disorder, is a deep, consistent fear of being scrutinized by people around you. This fear can appear in every environment—work, home, school, or even in public around strangers. Your brain's natural response is to keep you safe; in evolutionary terms, there is power and safety in numbers. If you were kicked out of the tribe in ancient times, you were left unprotected against predators and would likely not survive very long. If you have this core fear, even imagining being in a situation where you are at risk of embarrassment (e.g., speaking up in a meeting) is enough to give you heart palpitations and sweaty palms. Now, imagine if you simultaneously dream of sharing your ideas or art with the world; you can see why this would conflict with your need to avoid judgment from others.

#7. Fear of the unknown

Also known as the fear of change, this fear will cause you to believe that anything unknown or uncertain will lead to something worse and more painful than your current circumstances. People who suffer from this fear seek absolute certainty before making a decision or taking action. Even then, they often don't budge because there's still that glimmer of possibility that they won't be able to control the outcome. This fear usually stems from trauma in childhood, leading to a distrust in your loved ones' ability to keep you safe. It can also come from a parent who carried this fear and exhibited anxious behaviors about change and transition. This fear will keep you on the hamster wheel of life—so afraid to get off and experience anything different because you're uncertain of the outcome.

I say this with love: Your fears are *not unique.*

Your fears are not yours alone; most people carry one or more of these fears. Please hear me when I say your fears are not bigger than *you.* They are a part of your story up until now, but how you perceive and approach your fear is critical. Rather than resisting and pushing against it, experiencing your fear and overcoming it is an integral part of your growth here on Earth—it's part of the mystical curriculum we were all assigned at birth.

First, you have to pick up the mirror and look deeply into the face of your fear. Your fears are like the monsters under your bed from childhood—the product of an overactive imagination that is being used in the negative. It's time to turn the light on so you can see the illusions you've created for what they are.

HOW TO MANAGE YOUR FEARS

Identify

Just as a doctor needs to assess your symptoms before confirming a diagnosis, you must identify and name the fears you carry before deciding on a plan of action. You have to know what you're dealing with, which means you have to stop being afraid of your fear. What you resist persists. Your hate of this fear is only breeding more of it. You must first accept that you have it before you can let it go.

I bet you have a good enough read on your body that when you notice the first sign of swollen glands, sore throat, and stuffy nose, you diagnose an oncoming cold or flu. What about when you're feeling stressed-out, overwhelmed, or anxious about an upcoming experience? Can you identify which fear of yours is triggered at that moment?

The uncomfortable symptoms of a triggered fear are just feedback. It doesn't mean you're weak and pathetic, and it's certainly not another reason to shame and criticize yourself. The best action you can take is to name and claim it. As you create a list of your fears, do so from an honest, neutral space. This approach will allow you to take the next step and become an investigator of your own fear.

Investigate

It's time to start peeling back the layers of your fears. This is crucial because you must dismantle the subjective opinions your mind has been positioning as facts. That may sound daunting, but armed with the powerful questions that follow, you can crack the program of your current belief system and allow the light of truth to shine.

- Is this fear coming from a *real* threat, or is it self-created? If it's self-created, when is the first time I remember having the fear, and where did it come from?
- Is it possible that I've misperceived an experience? Am I assuming my past will be my future?
- Is it possible that what I fear isn't true? How does my body respond when I think of this fearful thought?

As you study your fears, take notes in your journal. Writing this information down will allow you to become the observer instead of perpetually reacting; every time you do this, you will create separation between yourself and your fear.

Create a new vision

A potential future exists in which you don't carry these self-created, illusory fears. The act of transforming your fears will alter your destiny in ways you can't possibly comprehend. It's yours to claim if you so choose, but you need to start by imagining something different for yourself so you can stop allowing your past to dictate your future.

- What would it feel like to live without this fear?
- What behaviors would change?
- What outcomes would I produce?
- If I woke up tomorrow without this fear, what would I do differently?

Get clear on your new vision so you can understand what's at stake if you *don't* do the work to resolve and release the fears that have held you back.

CLARIFY YOUR FEAR MANAGEMENT PLAN

It's not a matter of whether fear will show up on your journey to expressing your purpose—it's a matter of *when.*

I recommend you plan how to manage that fear so it doesn't become an immovable obstacle. Fear left untreated over time can cause emotional and mental stress, resulting in severe anxiety and panic attacks. It can also wreak havoc on your physical body. According to the National Library of Medicine, chronic stress adversely affects almost every system in the body. Stress is a leading cause of death in the United States by various effects including heart disease, cancer, liver cirrhosis, accidents, and suicide.

What follows are a few powerful suggestions for managing fear and stress when you meet them—as you inevitably will along this journey.

Be where your feet are

If you find yourself experiencing heightened fear, you are likely focused on fearful thoughts about your past or future. The present moment is the golden land of peace, where your power lives. As such, you need to become refocused in the *present.* You can do this through meditation, deep breathing, yoga, or even taking a walk. If you're in a meeting, put your hands on your desk and silently repeat: *I am here.* A quick reminder is to always be where your feet are, not where they were or will be.

Talk it out

This one was tough for me. I believed my fears would magically disappear if I ignored them long enough. Well, I was wrong. I was ashamed of my fears and didn't want to let on that I had any, so I kept them hidden. However, what I couldn't hide was my behavior. Behavior is the great revealer. When it came time for me to step out in the world and be seen, procrastination, perfectionism, and self-sabotage repeatedly got in my way. It wasn't until I was willing to talk about it that those behaviors shifted into the positive.

Find someone to talk to when you feel overwhelmed and disempowered by fear. You can choose a mental health professional, coach, partner, or best friend. Whomever you choose, trust this person enough to go there and to share how you're feeling and what you're thinking. When you say out loud what's in your head and your heart, you're perfectly poised to shift how you perceive the issue, as long as you intend to let it go.

What you choose to hide, you choose to keep.

Rudi and I are each other's sounding board. Every evening after work, we sit outside to unwind and share how our day went. We both share our feelings and any challenges we encountered throughout the day. Generally, just speaking it out loud diminishes any negative emotion I'm experiencing. Then, with Rudi's help, I can reframe how I perceive the issue.

Reconnect to your why

When you start to create change, it will feel foreign and uncomfortable. It'll be tempting to retreat back into past routines and habits that feel familiar.

Your *why* needs to be your emergency life-saving device and should be stronger than the need to be comfortable.

Ask yourself the following questions when you start to feel fear:

- Why am I taking this action?
- What's at stake?
- What will I feel if I *don't* achieve my dream or desire? And what will I feel if I *do*?
- How will achieving my dream positively affect others?

Ask yourself these same questions every damn day if you have to. Just don't turn back!

TAKE ACTION

You can spend a lifetime dancing around your fear, finding ways to avoid it or live with it—or you can decide to walk through it. The antidote to fear is taking action and doing what you most fear. As American writer and lecturer Dale Carnegie so eloquently said, "Inaction breeds doubt and fear. Action breeds confidence and courage. If you want to conquer fear, do not sit home and think about it. Do go out and get busy."

This step is arguably the hardest because it's where the rubber meets the road. Moving through the fear illusion requires taking action. It will require you to take a few steps out of your comfort zone and do the very thing you've been avoiding. For example, if you fear public speaking, look for a local Toastmasters organization in your community or ask your boss if you can kick off the next board meeting.

Managing your fear is not a once-and-done activity (I wish!). It's an essential daily practice. It took you a lifetime to develop and nurture your fears, so it will take time and work to dismantle and dissolve them. What I know to be true is that when you start to experience the benefits of this work, it becomes something you *want* to do instead of something you *should* do.

A quote commonly attributed to my favorite poet Ralph Waldo Emerson is "He who is not every day conquering some fear has not learned the secret of life." Stepping out of your comfort zone intentionally is the bridge to freedom and living a beautiful, fulfilling, successful life.

Love is real; fear is not. Love yourself, your life, and your purpose enough that there is no room left for fear. Love always wins.

PUTTING IT INTO PRACTICE

Pick one of the fears you've identified. Take your fear through the steps outlined in this chapter:

1. Identify: What is the underlying fear causing your negative symptoms?
2. Investigate: Is this fear based on truth or your imagination?
3. Create a new vision: What would life look like without this fear?
4. Create your fear management plan: What are you going to do when this fear shows up? How can you make it so this fear doesn't stop you anymore?
5. Take action: What action can you take that will serve to transform this fear?

Chapter 6

UPGRADE YOUR BELIEFS

If you accept a limiting belief, then it will become true for you.

—Louise Hay, American Motivational Speaker and Author

"GIVE ME YOUR SUNGLASSES; THEY are so dirty I don't know how you see through them!"

That's what Rudi says to me almost every morning as we set out on our daily four-mile walk. I'm not sure why my sunglasses can't seem to stay clean. It probably has to do with my habit of throwing them in my purse without a case and the sticky fingers of my kids, who love to play with my things.

Yet, I'll put them on, dirty fingerprints and all, and wear them for hours before my husband snatches them off my face to give them a good cleaning. After he's done, I'll put them back on and think: *Wow—what a difference. Everything looks clear and bright.*

So, why is it that I can't be aware enough to clean my glasses? Why do I need someone else to bring it to my attention?

It turns out that when you wear dirty lenses long enough, you don't notice they're dirty anymore; it just becomes your norm.

I once read a quote by Stephen Covey, American businessman, educator, and bestselling author of *The 7 Habits of Highly Effective People*, which dramatically transformed my way of thinking. Covey writes, "We must look at the lens through which we see the world as well as the world we see, and understand that the lens itself shapes how we interpret the world."

Is it possible that the lens I'm wearing to view the world differs from yours? Do I see an opportunity where you see a challenge? Do I see abundance where you see lack? Do I see love and protection where you see fear and danger?

This chapter is about the lens you have worn up until now and how you can give it a good cleaning so that you can see yourself, your purpose, and your mission more clearly.

The invisible lens you wear is made up of your beliefs about yourself and the world.

The good news is that some of your beliefs are positive and supportive of what you want to experience—such as the belief that you have excellent health or are worthy of a deep, meaningful, loving relationship. Those beliefs would color your lens, allowing you to see and experience more of that in your life.

But what about the negative, limiting beliefs we hold about ourselves? How do we clear that lens to see and experience something different—something better?

When I coach individuals who want to achieve an important dream or desire but can't seem to make it happen, I like to give them the analogy of a minefield.

Imagine you are standing on one side of a big open field. On the other side of the field, near a beautiful clearing of trees, is the completion of your goal or the manifestation of your desire. Now, you start taking one step after another toward that clearing. But then, out of nowhere, you step on a trigger. There's an explosion and you feel pain, fear, and panic. You realize it's a minefield and you don't know where the others are buried. You have a choice; you can run back to where you started and never venture out toward your dream again, or you can take a deep breath, allow the pain to move through you, and move forward, knowing you will invariably step on another trigger.

The minefield is symbolic of your limiting beliefs and the fears associated with them. Any time you step out of your comfort zone (which is generally required to expand and do something you've never done), you risk getting majorly triggered and coming up against the feelings, emotions, and experiences you've spent your whole life avoiding.

We're taught to avoid physical, mental, and emotional pain at all costs. The problem is that to move through, transform, and release our limiting beliefs about what we think is possible, we *must* walk through that field.

To do the work to evolve, grow, and heal, we must have a big enough carrot to force us outside of our comfort zone. And the carrots in this metaphor are your most profound dreams and desires. What if your wishes, those on the other side of that minefield, are just there to force you to keep walking forward so you can see the explosions for the illusions they really are?

The idea that you can't do or aren't good at certain things is bullshit, for the most part. You don't have to live in the prison of your limitations—so let's get busy being *limitless.*

WHAT ARE LIMITING BELIEFS?

Limiting beliefs are false thoughts and opinions that one holds to be the absolute truth. They are assumptions about your reality that come from your *perceptions* of life experiences, and they will stop you from moving forward and growing personally.

There are external limiting beliefs about how the world works and what is possible, and then there are internal limiting beliefs (better known as self-limiting beliefs) that relate to your identity, what you're capable of, and what is possible for you.

Self-limiting beliefs often come disguised in sentences that start with "I can't" or "I'm not." For example: "I'm not smart enough for that job"; "I can't lose weight, no matter what I do"; "I'm not capable of making more money"; "I'm not qualified enough"; "I'm not beautiful enough"; or "I can't pursue my dreams because I may fail."

Any of that sound familiar? We all carry them.

HOW DO SELF-LIMITING BELIEFS FORM?

Think of your brain as a supercomputer; the beliefs you form are like a computer operating system. Once installed, this program runs behind the scenes 24 hours a day, 365 days a year.

This belief program then acts as a filter for what information will make it to your conscious mind, impacting your decisions in subtle yet significant ways.

Here's a fun fact: With your five senses, your human body perceives and sends 11 million bits of information per second to the brain, but only 50 bits per second make it to your conscious mind. And what determines the information that you become aware of?

You got it—it's your beliefs.

Some beliefs are positive and help us create better lives. But some act as false barriers that prevent us from reaching our highest potential.

WHERE DO LIMITING BELIEFS COME FROM?

Dr. Bruce Lipton, the author of the bestselling book *The Biology of Belief*, claims that until age seven or eight, our brains operate in a subconscious hypnotic state, which means we are highly suggestible. In this state, children are like video cameras, recording everything they observe. Most of our limiting beliefs are formed during this time as we subconsciously process what happens outside of us and absorb it as fact. Our brains are a blank canvas in this period, just waiting to be filled with beliefs. So, we often absorb the beliefs of others, or we base our beliefs on how we perceive (and often misperceive) experiences.

Let me give you an example of how this works. I want you to imagine being six years old and bullied by your classmates at school. Every time the teacher calls on you, you give the wrong answer; the kids giggle and call you stupid, causing you to feel intense shame and humiliation. This scene is repeated a few times throughout the school year, and you start to think they might be right, that not knowing the correct answers means you're stupid. Your brain then forms a program called "I'm not smart," and it begins to run 24/7.

Part of your brain's function is to form and maintain beliefs. Psychologists describe this as "belief perseverance," or your brain's cognitive bias for filtering out information that does not confirm your existing beliefs. Essentially, your brain always brings you information to substantiate what you already believe.

Moving forward with that limiting belief of "I'm not smart," if you were to pass nine tests but fail one, you would likely highlight the one failed test as evidence that you are unintelligent instead of perceiving the nine passed tests as evidence to the contrary.

Your belief about not being smart becomes the rope around your neck, holding you back from fully applying yourself, taking risks, or moving toward new opportunities. You could spend a lifetime tethered to that restrictive belief because you don't even know it's there; you believe this is just the way you are, and there's nothing you can do to change it!

American self-help author, coach, and speaker Tony Robbins says, "All personal breakthrough begins with a change in beliefs." I couldn't agree more. Through actively releasing limiting beliefs—the very one I lay out for you in this chapter—I have created a successful career, up-leveled my relationships, and achieved goals that I once considered impossible. I have also been able to pursue my purpose, knowing that I can change my beliefs to *support* my dreams.

But let's be clear: I wasn't always this way.

I was an incredibly insecure child, and one of the many limiting beliefs I had formed was that I was incapable of public speaking. I realize "incapable" is a strong word, but that's precisely how I felt.

It all started when I was ten, and my teacher asked the entire class to prepare and present a report on different countries. I came to class prepared, but something happened as I watched each classmate get up and take their turn at the podium. My heart started beating incredibly fast; my palms got sweaty; my thoughts became scattered, and I began to have what I now know was a panic attack.

At that moment, I heard my teacher announce that it was my turn. As I fumbled to get out of my seat, it felt like my legs were made of lead. I tried to pick up my report and poster board, but my hands shook so badly that I could barely hold on to them. I finally managed to make it up to the podium. When I looked up from my script and saw all the kids in the class staring, waiting for me to say something, I lost my ability to speak. I couldn't even utter a sound.

Seeing what was happening, my teacher approached the podium and whispered, "Are you okay?"

I shook my head no, and she said, "Why don't you sit down, and we can do this later?"

I grabbed my things and returned to my desk, refusing to make eye contact with anyone because I was too ashamed and embarrassed. I didn't want to see my failure and shame validated in their eyes.

From that moment onward, I made a silent pact that I would never put myself in that position again. I began rearranging my life to avoid feeling the horrible panic and humiliation I would surely experience again if forced to speak in front of the class.

I called in sick on presentation days, chose classes without public speaking components, and made a million excuses to my teachers. I let avoiding that fear become a priority and successfully did so for ten years.

During my sophomore year at Texas Christian University, I declared my major in Advertising. I dreamed of working at a cool, hip advertising agency when I graduated; the one at the top of my list was coming to recruit at my school.

I sat in the audience, watching them present the fantastic campaigns they had released for world-renowned brands and listening to them talk about their unique agency culture, and every cell in my body lit up. I *knew* this was the perfect agency for me.

I felt totally aligned with every word that came out of the speaker's mouth—until they turned to their last slide listing off the requirements for applicants. And coming in at number one on the list: must be a proficient and compelling public speaker.

My heart sank, and my eyes welled with tears. I couldn't understand how this dream I held could be gone in a heartbeat. I believed there was no way I would ever be able to stand up on a stage and present as they had just done, which meant there was no way I would get the job.

I walked out of the auditorium, and rather than rush off to my next class, I found a quiet bench to sit on and think about what had just happened. I immediately started to brainstorm ways around this public speaking requirement. I could find another department to work in at the agency, or maybe I needed to change my major to accounting and be done with it.

But each option felt wrong because it would require me to walk away from my dream of being a successful account executive, overseeing major brand campaigns at a big, sexy advertising agency. At this moment, I heard a little voice inside my head that said, "What if you *could* be a great public speaker?" I immediately brushed it off because that seemed *impossible*. But I had to admit that it was the best option I had come up with while sitting on that bench. I allowed myself to return to that possibility and thought: *What if I could become a capable public speaker?*

Instantly, I felt a little glimmer of hope. Because if there was even a 1 percent chance that I could get over my fear of public speaking, there was a 1 percent chance I could still achieve my dream.

I got up from that bench, marched my ass to the registrar's office, and changed my minor to speech communication. I became a woman on a mission.

I received my syllabus, scheduled private appointments with my new professors to explain my fears, and asked for their support and guidance. I read books, took additional courses outside of school, and spent the next two years doing whatever I had to do to become a proficient and compelling public speaker.

Not only did I get accepted into that agency's competitive internship program during my junior year of college, but they also offered me a full-time account executive position on a high-profile account before I graduated.

Little did I know then that every subsequent job opportunity would come not *despite* my perceived limitation but *because* I had summoned the courage to disprove my prior limiting belief. I went on to leave that agency after a few years so I could travel the world and become a professional public speaker.

What if I had chosen my limitation over my dream at that moment on the bench?

I return to that moment every time I'm faced with a tough choice, reminding myself that nothing good comes from protecting my limitations.

Your beliefs about what you *can* and *can't* do drive your behavior.

But here's the good news: When the need to change becomes greater than the fear of addressing your limiting belief, you are ready.

Just as you programmed your beliefs through your agreement with them, you can choose to deconstruct them and declare you no longer abide by their limits. As American writer Richard Bach says, "If you argue for your limitations, they are yours."

WHERE DO YOU START?

So, now that you know you have limiting beliefs (we all do), you get to choose whether you will remove them or hold on to them for safekeeping.

It's always a choice. And it's yours to make. But if you desire to create any positive change in your life, you have to be ready to clean off the lens of your worldview.

So, if you're game, I will take you through a process to identify what you want and the limiting beliefs standing in your way. The following exercise is based on a workshop I'm often asked to host at conferences and new hire trainings. It sparks profound transformation and aha moments as long as you go all in and take some time to contemplate.

Step 1: Why do you want what you want?

Whether we achieve our goals depends on commitment and action. But what determines whether we take action? It's how motivated we are! And to achieve peak motivation, you must be clear on your why.

- What is one of your greatest dreams or desires?
- Why do you want to achieve this dream?
- What will the achievement of that dream give you?
- What will this achievement help you feel?

Step 2: What limiting belief is standing in your way?

There's always a limiting belief masquerading as an excuse for why we can't achieve the things we want. Answer the following questions to highlight the limiting belief you feel is the biggest obstacle to your success.

- What reasons/excuses do you have for not achieving your goals so far?
- What's the limiting belief behind those reasons?

For example, let's say your goal is to buy a home. Your reason for not achieving that goal might be insufficient money. The limiting belief behind that reason is "I believe I can't make enough money to buy a home."

Step 3: How accurate is the belief?

A belief is only a thought you keep thinking—a narrative our mind builds to define who we are and what we're capable of. But an uninvestigated belief can wreak great havoc on our lives.

Revisiting the story I shared, I was a ten-year-old who let one experience define who I was and what I was capable of for years after that. But what if I was mistaken all along? Is it possible that I hadn't had the experience to be a proficient public speaker? Could it have been that I panicked because I was young and didn't have the self-esteem I do now? Is it possible that I perceived that experience incorrectly, and I could be good at public speaking now? Or learn to be?

Now, it's time for you to investigate your own limiting beliefs. Answer the following questions:

- Do you know the limiting belief you identified is 100 percent true?
- Could you prove it in a court of law?
- What evidence is there to prove that your belief might not be true?

Step 4: What is it costing you?

Your limiting belief is costing you way more than you think. The collateral damage of our limiting beliefs can be catastrophic; they affect not only our lives but also the lives of those close to us. If I hadn't gotten over my limiting belief about my ability to speak in public, I wouldn't have gotten the job I wanted, jumped at the opportunity to work as a professional speaker on cruise ships, had the chance to make a lot of money and travel the world, and met my husband at a cruise industry conference.

And most importantly, I would have missed the opportunity to show myself how powerful I am and that I can overcome any limitation.

I want you to travel back in time to identify when your limiting belief started. Become the observer of how this belief has affected your life, and answer the following questions.

- What are the harmful effects of this belief?
- What has it cost you? What opportunities have you missed because of it?
- How would you feel right now if you didn't have the limiting belief?
- How would your life look different now without that belief?

Step 5: Make the commitment

So, here we are—it's decision time. Based on the exercise we have just done, are you still in agreement with this limiting belief? Does it serve you and your mission? Does it make you feel empowered and expansive, or does it make you feel weak and small?

If you no longer accept your limiting belief (which I really hope is the case), here are techniques to help you transform and release it.

CHANGE YOUR LANGUAGE

One of the most effective ways to shut down old limiting belief programs is to shift how you speak. By inserting a few powerful words into your language, you can create enough disruption in your thought patterns to start dismantling limitations, piece by piece.

For example, one of the most powerful three-letter words on the planet is *yet*. Instead of saying, "I can't lose weight," say, "I can't lose weight *yet*." Or, "I can't speak another language" can shift into "I can't speak another language *yet*." Do you see the difference in how that feels?

Another excellent limiting belief disruptor is to change "I can't" to "How can I?" or "I'm not" to "How can I be?" This technique is called Socratic questioning. It is a powerful cognitive restructuring technique that can help you challenge irrational or harmful thoughts. When you say, "I can't," your brain will give you information validating that belief. It's time to start programming your brain to look for possibility, not impossibility. When you change limiting, declarative statements like "I can't" to "How can I?" you are reprogramming your brain to look for solutions instead of accepting failure. This exercise is an excellent start to training your brain to look for possibilities.

PROVE YOURSELF WRONG (AND DO IT OFTEN)

A powerful way to break limiting beliefs is to make a habit of doing things you never thought you could do. Your limiting beliefs keep you in your comfort zone.

Success *won't be found* in your comfort zone.

I'm a big fan of endurance training, and one year I completed a half-marathon. I didn't take on this goal because of the few steps I would take over the finish line. I did it because every Saturday for five months, I got to stretch my belief of what was possible. Each week, the distance would get farther, and I would have to do the thing I had never done. And every time, I would prove to myself that I could!

Achieving this goal started a chain reaction of questions in my mind: What else is possible? Where else can I prove myself wrong in what I have believed I couldn't do? In my relationships? In my career? In my health?

Hear this: *Competence* breeds *confidence.*

Many people want to feel confident in something they haven't been willing to become competent in. How do you start to become competent? Read books on the topic, take courses, find a mentor who has achieved what you want to achieve, and spend time daily focusing on practicing and applying what you learn.

TAKE ACCOUNTABILITY

According to a study by the American Society of Training and Development, you are 65 percent more likely to achieve a goal if you've declared your commitment to achieving it to someone else. Even better, if you assign a specific individual to hold you accountable to completion, you will increase your chance of success to 95 percent.

Share your goal to release your limiting beliefs with someone. Make it public and put some skin in the game. Find someone you trust, someone who will stand for your vision, and someone you won't quickly sell out on or make excuses to. Make a list of actions you are committing to complete and check in with your accountability partner.

As Dr. Wayne Dyer so eloquently stated, "There is one grand lie—that we are limited. The only limits we have are the limits we believe." You are not limited. You have negative beliefs about yourself that were created by misperceiving events and experiences in your childhood. That's it—no shame or blame in that. There's no reason to feel regret or guilt. We've *all* done it.

As you step fully into your mission, path, and purpose, you will bump up against these limiting beliefs, but instead of running back to old ways of being, be grateful for them. If you didn't know they were there, you couldn't transform them into something better.

When people ask me how long it takes to courageously move forward with their life purpose, I answer that it's directly proportional to their willingness to release limiting beliefs that cause the traffic jams in their forward movement.

So, do the work, and you'll reap the reward of true freedom.

PUTTING IT INTO PRACTICE

Right now, write down one action you can take toward proving your limiting belief wrong—something you can do *today*. Now commit to it. Share what action you will take with someone you trust and then report back once it's complete.

Chapter 7

RELEASE IMPOSTER SYNDROME

The best advice I've ever received is, 'No one else knows what they're doing either.'

—Ricky Gervais, English Comedian, Actor, Writer, Producer, and Director

IN THE SPRING OF 2020, COVID-19 shut down the world, and I was furloughed from my job. Rather than sit and wallow in self-pity, I decided to use the time to get my coaching certification and build a coaching business with Rudi. I had wanted to do this for quite a while but had never found the time. And at that point, while stuck in my house, I had all the time in the world.

I'll never forget my first day of sales calls as a newbie coach. Rudi and I had offered complimentary coaching calls to our email list, and I had a full calendar. My expectations were high with the goal of facilitating groundbreaking aha moments for these individuals and enrolling those who were a good fit into one of our coaching programs.

I had experience coaching. Acting as a mentor and counselor for my family, friends, and colleagues came as naturally to me as breathing. What was new to me was *charging* for my services. I had never questioned my ability to coach. I had done so unofficially for years and had even taken on some pro-bono clients and bartered services with others. But the second I assigned a price tag to it, my self-doubt came fast and furious.

I had effectively avoided having to sell my services by adopting beliefs like "I don't have enough time in my schedule" or "My website and messaging need to be tweaked (for the fiftieth time)." I eventually accepted the fact that coaching would always remain a hobby until I had paying clients.

I was nervous and excited as I dialed in for my first enrollment call. It was with a woman who felt unfulfilled in her job and wanted to align with her calling to be a spiritual teacher. This topic was in my wheelhouse, so the nerves disappeared, and I poured into her for over an hour. I helped her identify where she was getting stuck, clarify her unique gifts and purpose, and commit to a few action steps to get her started. We were both elated! I knew I could guide her in creating her vision and that she would need support to ensure she didn't let her fears take over. Yet, when it came time for me to invite her to enroll in my program, I lost all confidence, danced around the price, and failed to confidently communicate the results I could envision for her. I totally bombed.

Unfortunately, the next call went the same, as did the one after that. By the end of the day, I felt utterly deflated and was ready to throw in the towel. All the individuals I spoke to were so grateful for my time and even sent thank you emails to share their praise. Yet they all felt like it wasn't the right time to enroll or that they didn't have the financial means to do so.

That evening, I sat in a deep well of inadequacy, creating the story that they had all seen through me and recognized that I wasn't good enough to impact their lives. I felt like a complete fraud. Then, I heard a little voice in my head that said, "I will never enroll someone in my program until I first enroll *myself.*" Damn, that was a punch in the gut.

I couldn't blame these women for declining my enrollment offer because at that point, I wouldn't have signed up for my services either.

This experience created a profound shift for me because I realized I had skipped a pivotal step in showing up for my calling as a spiritual teacher and mentor. I had failed to ensure I fully believed in my ability to create an impact. I had yet to enroll myself in the value I bring and the past experiences that had qualified me for the role. You can't fake energy, and the potential clients I had spoken to could sense my lack of confidence about offering my services for a fee.

Rudi and I see this same situation play out with almost every purpose-driven entrepreneur we have worked with. You have to buy into the value you offer as a prerequisite to getting others to buy it. Even if your goal is more personal than professional, there will come a point when you need to enroll your spouse, friends, boss, or potential partners in your vision. To do that, you must fully *believe* in your mission, which will require you to overcome your imposter syndrome.

WHAT IS IMPOSTER SYNDROME?

Imposter syndrome is a psychological condition characterized by doubt concerning one's abilities or accomplishments, accompanied by the fear of being exposed as a fraud and a fake despite evidence of the contrary.

This affliction doesn't discriminate by age, gender, race, or financial status. Some of society's most well-known and affluent people have spoken openly about experiencing debilitating imposter syndrome. Michelle Obama, the two-term First Lady of the United States, said, "I still have a little impostor syndrome . . . It doesn't go away, that feeling that you shouldn't take me seriously. What do I know? I share that with you because we all have doubt in our abilities, about our power, and what that power is."

If Michelle Obama suffers from imposter syndrome, how are the rest of us supposed to cope?

Hand to heart, I confess I have experienced the feeling of being an *imposter* at the beginning of almost everything I have ever done. I felt like an imposter in middle school art class, on my first shift as a waitress, my first day of college, my first real job as an account executive, the first fifty times I stepped onstage to host an event on a cruise ship, the first year of being a mother, throughout every single promotion I have ever received, and definitely the first time I decided to write a book.

The common symptoms of imposter syndrome are an overarching

doubt in your capabilities, gifts, success, and achievements; a fear of being exposed as a fake and a fraud; and a belief that you are not good enough or as capable as others. These symptoms cause self-sabotaging behavior like procrastination, perfectionism, noncompletion, and manifestation of all sorts of distractions.

Nothing, and I mean *nothing,* will exacerbate your internal case of imposter syndrome like the journey to fulfilling your calling. This is when your mind and heart get in the boxing ring and take hits at each other—your mind throwing a mean cross of, "You aren't qualified or good enough, and this is a horrible, no good, terrible idea," and your heart throwing an uppercut saying, "You *are* perfectly prepared and qualified, otherwise, you would not have the desire in the first place; and guess what, it is not going away."

The good news is that just by reading this chapter, you can get the upper hand as you become aware of how imposter syndrome (working like a puppet master behind the scenes) keeps you from fully stepping into your purpose.

HOW IS IMPOSTER SYNDROME SHOWING UP FOR YOU?

Imposter syndrome can be treated, but first, you need to understand how it uniquely presents itself in your situation.

1. Observe your thoughts and the voice in your head. Do any of the following thoughts come up for you? If so, take note of the ones you hear most frequently and under what circumstances they pop into your awareness.
    - I feel like a fake and a fraud.
    - I'm not good enough.
    - Who am I to do this?
    - I don't know how to do this.
    - This won't last.
    - I can't charge someone for this.

- I've just gotten lucky.
- I won't be able to live up to their expectations.
- I don't deserve this.

2. Observe your behaviors and forms of self-sabotage. What do you do when any of these thoughts enter your mind? Remember, your actions are inspired by the thoughts you think.

What follows are some behaviors common to those suffering from imposter syndrome. Take note of all that relate to you. Be honest with yourself (no blame, shame, or guilt required).

Perfectionism

Individuals who demonstrate perfectionism can be described as "control freaks" or "micro-managers." They believe if they want something done right, they have to do it on their own. What's going on below the surface is they don't feel good enough, but they can pretend to be fine as long as their work is flawless. They *become* the work, and any imperfection in it validates their fears of being inadequate.

Perfectionism will cause you to get so caught up in the details that moving forward becomes nearly impossible; you end up stressing over every little social media post, re-filming a simple video over and over, and worrying that your branding still isn't quite right. Perfectionism will lead to forever chasing your tail and burning yourself out without getting anywhere. It is a trap without a door because perfection doesn't exist. The only way out is to accept that what you create is *good enough* so that you can move on.

Overworking

Are you that person who believes downtime is a waste of time? Do you arrive to work earlier and stay later than your colleagues? Do you feel your value to your employer and business equates to the hours you clock and the work you produce? Do you believe success only comes to those who work hard for it? Overworking is a common symptom of imposter syndrome, mainly because society elevates and heralds those who work the *hardest* to achieve their goals.

Here's the thing: It doesn't have to be challenging unless you believe it has to be. This misbelief is the worst part of this particular symptom, as your beliefs and expectations create your reality. For you, every bit of success probably has required a commitment to doing, doing, doing.

The behavior of overworking comes from the thought that you are not enough, so you must prove your worth by doing, and if you're not doing work, then you are not worthy. I have worked with people who seem to create a shitstorm of work for themselves. They will take on too much work, agree to unrealistic deadlines, and then fight through the stress and anxiety, staying up all night and trying to get it all done. Their standard answer to "How are you?" is "Busy!" But they are choosing this way of being. Busyness is an intimacy issue. If you stack your plate too high with a million things to do, you don't have to ever *be* with yourself, sit with the negative emotions, and deal with the areas in your life that need addressing.

Procrastination

Oh, procrastination, how are you, my old friend? This unhealthy behavior was my go-to for many, many years. I'm a type-A Capricorn who loves to make to-do lists and check off completed items with a sparkly pen. I loved creating business plans and breaking down every milestone into small, achievable tasks. But somehow, the tasks that were most important for me to focus on were the ones that were left unchecked at the end of the day. These were often self-driven desires for which I didn't have anyone holding a hard and fast deadline over my head. It was easy to push them off to a later date. The problem is that for many of these tasks, later never came, and the entire desire would eventually be scrapped.

Let's look at what was really going on. My actions were in response to a fear of failure and of being seen. If I never completed something, I was at no risk of feeling the icky emotions of humiliation, judgment, and rejection. While my heart guided me to create impactful content, books, and courses, my mind was sabotaging those efforts with thoughts like, "Will delaying another day make a difference?" or "You're tired and have worked hard. You don't need to write today." Our minds are super sneaky that way! It is like watching a movie and discovering one of the supporting characters you thought was a good guy is turning out to be a lying cheat with evil intentions all along. I hate to be the bearer of bad news, but your mind is not always your friend. But it *can be* convinced to work on your side when you treat it like a child and know it doesn't always make the best decisions.

Refusing to ask for help

Have you ever thought that if you have to ask for help, then you must not be qualified to do what you're doing? Do you believe asking for help is a weakness, and all those people who need to take classes and courses to learn are just phonies trying to be something they're not?

Did you come out of the womb knowing how to speak, write, read, solve complex math equations, and change a light bulb? No—you learned from your parents, siblings, teachers, friends, and neighbors. Why on earth would you think you should magically know everything there is to know about a topic without asking for help? I have seen many purpose-driven entrepreneurs fall prey to not asking for help. It's hard to watch them struggle with something that could be resolved in seconds if they asked someone who knows the answer!

I remember the first time I tried reconciling our business account in QuickBooks. I was so lost that I made a mess of everything. I must have struggled for *days* to figure out what each tab and function meant and how to ensure everything was reconciling correctly. Finally, after many failed attempts, I hired someone to do it for me for $50. Literally, within an hour, I had my reconciliation report ready to send to my accountant, and it was *perfect.* If left undetected, this behavior can stop you from fulfilling your purpose before you even start. Along this journey you will encounter so many things you don't know how to do. Each time you come up against one of them, be willing to ask for help from someone who does know!

Turning down opportunities

Have you ever said no to an opportunity because you did not feel ready? Do you shy away from trying something new and stick to the things you excel at? This behavior is 100 percent because your fear of failure is overtaking your desire for a more meaningful life. Guess what—you are *never* going to feel ready and fully prepared. That is, you won't feel that way until you do the thing you're not great at enough times. It's only through experience that we learn.

You can read every book on a topic. But you haven't fully learned until you apply the information somehow. For instance, Rudi and I coach individuals to become confident and compelling public speakers. Do we just let them sit across from us and take notes so they know how to do it someday? Nope! We make them get up on the stage and present over and over and over again. Generally, the first time is not great, but with repetition and practice, they improve. Imposter syndrome can cause you to never feel ready for what you are meant to do. Yet, the Universe will lovingly send you opportunities to prove yourself wrong. You have to commit to saying, "What the hell, I'll do it!"

Thinking it's never good enough

Do you feel whatever you do is never good enough? Do you criticize yourself after a presentation or after finishing a project for not making it better or showing up differently?

Rudi struggled with this after every presentation and live training he hosted. At first, he would feel excited and energized, having shown up to do what he loves to do. But then the doubt would set in, and he would question if it was impactful enough. He would want to watch the recording, not to improve his performance, but to look for all the mistakes. We most often think of imposter syndrome as what happens before we take action, but it can also show up *after.* If you let this symptom continue, it will eventually affect your willingness to take risks and say yes to opportunities as they come. I recommend adopting the belief that as long as you do your best, that is enough. You also must ask yourself what you're committed to. Are you committed to creating an impact for someone else, or are you committed to making sure you look good and impress others?

Inability to accept praise

What do you say when someone congratulates you or offers you a compliment? Do you say, "Thank you," or try convincing them that their praise was unfounded? I think women suffer from this particular imposter symptom more than men. Sheryl Sandberg, the former chief operating officer of Facebook and bestselling author of *Lean In*, explained that many people, especially women, feel fraudulent when praised for their accomplishments. Instead of feeling worthy of recognition, they feel undeserving and guilty, as if a mistake has been made.

Why is it so much easier for men to accept praise than women? It's because men are supposed to appear confident and capable, even when they aren't. Women are taught the opposite, to appear humble and low-key, so they tend to deflect.

This inability to accept praise is 100 percent a worthiness issue. If you don't do the work to elevate your self-worth, you will always feel this way, no matter how high you climb up the corporate ladder, how many books you write, or the lives you transform. I think this inability to accept praise stems from a resistance to receive. Women are very comfortable in the giving role; when you give to another, you get a nice dopamine hit from feeling valued and affirmed that you have a place in this world. Women are expected to wear multiple hats and juggle too many balls with a smile—spouse, kids, house, activities, trips, jobs, philanthropies, and more. At what point will we be able to receive assistance and accept compliments on a job well done without discounting and measuring our work in a perfectionistic way?

So, which of these symptoms do you relate to? Do you experience one more than the other or all of them? It bears repeating: You are not alone. Everyone experiences these symptoms in one form or another. The good news is you get to heal the wounds that underlie impostor syndrome and all its related symptoms.

HOW TO COPE WITH IMPOSTER SYNDROME

1. **Become self-aware.**

   You need to observe every time you are experiencing a symptom. Rather than identify with it, ask yourself *why*. If you had a cold, you would not identify with your sneeze and assume it would always be there. You would know that it is a symptom of a virus and will be gone as soon as your cold medicine and immune system do their thing. I recommend you create a log sheet. Every time you experience a symptom of imposter syndrome, write down the details of your thoughts and what you did when they surfaced.

2. **Investigate your thoughts.**

   I am a big fan of Byron Katie's book *The Work of Byron Katie.* In it she presents a simple yet profound system for self-inquiry. Whenever you have a thought that creates a negative emotion, you can ask yourself questions that will allow you to investigate and eventually release the thought. I recommend you ask yourself the following questions:

   - Is the thought absolutely, beyond a shadow of a doubt, true?
   - How would I feel if I didn't have this thought?
   - Is there any positive reason for me to keep this thought?

3. **Up-level your inner narrative.**

   Creating time for daily affirmations is a powerful practice for reworking your inner narrative loop. If you identify a negative thought that keeps popping up, write it down. Then, rewrite the thought to make it positive. For example, if your negative thought is "I am not qualified to do this," flip the statement to be "I am getting more qualified every day," or "I am fully qualified and prepared to create an impact."

4. **Be kind to yourself.**
   It's important to remind yourself daily that everyone has doubts and fears, and you are not alone. I recommend reading memoirs and biographies written by individuals who have successfully created what you desire. You will quickly see that they also had to overcome their internal demons.

5. **Celebrate the big and small wins.**
   Instead of looking at how far you have left to go, regularly celebrate how far you have come. Even if the action you completed is as small as sending an email to a prospective client, it is worth celebrating! If you can focus on your forward movement instead of believing you are miles behind, you will feel better and be more apt to take the big leaps when required.

Ninety-nine percent of the readers who pick up this book can relate to experiencing some form of imposter syndrome, past and present. It's okay. You can go ahead and release all the self-blame and shame because it is a waste of your energy. It is a part of the human condition, but it is certainly not fixed. You can break through these negative behavior patterns with intention and commitment. When you do, you'll feel a sort of freedom you never knew existed!

PUTTING IT INTO PRACTICE

Write yourself a prescription to treat your imposter syndrome.

Remember, you are the doctor here, and imposter syndrome won't be cured overnight. It will require your attention and commitment to healing, one day at a time.

Based on the information and insights you have gained about how imposter syndrome shows up in your life, prescribe a plan for yourself. What do you recommend for *you*? As you journey beyond your comfort zone, negative thoughts will inevitably pop up. So, think through the actions you will take when you are triggered or when you fall back into old behaviors of perfectionism, procrastination, or some other symptom of self-doubt. Revisit this document as often as you need.

Chapter 8

STOP THE COMPARISON CYCLE

Comparison is the thief of joy.

—Anonymous

HAVE YOU EVER BEEN INSPIRED to do or create something only to discover others doing the same thing, and believed there was too much competition? Have you ever witnessed a colleague knock a presentation out of the park and think there's no way you'll ever match up to their talent, so why even try?

Comparison is the silent killer of soul-aligned dreams. You can't see, touch, or taste it. But suppose you crack the door open and let it in. Once it gets ahold of you, it can quickly act as a creative virus, deflating every ounce of confidence and hope that your desire might become a reality.

With the rise of social media, this silent killer has become an *epidemic.*

One of my former colleagues, Andrea, called one day to declare her intention to be a leadership coach. She was lit up from the inside out, and I couldn't help but join in on her excitement. She was currently working as an account executive at a large corporation and felt inspired to support other professionals to succeed in their careers and personal lives. This was her dream, and she said she wouldn't stop until she achieved it.

A few months passed, and I hadn't heard from Andrea, so I called her to check in on her progress. The woman who answered the phone sounded anything but excited; in fact, she sounded totally *defeated.* I wondered, *Oh no, what happened?*

To launch her coaching business, she had spent a lot of time online taking courses, reading articles on marketing, and researching other leadership coaches to see what their websites looked like, what they offered, and how they were communicating their services. What started as an innocent fact-finding mission sent her down a rabbit hole of checking these coaches' Instagram followers, Facebook posts, professional speaking reels, top podcast features, and press coverage from *Forbes* and the *New York Times.*

To Andrea, who had yet to sign her first client, they looked larger than life and at the top of their game. To make matters worse, so many established coaches seemed to be targeting the same demographic she was, and the clients were leaving review after raving review on their websites and social media pages. This was when her initial excitement started to morph into doubt and defeat.

She didn't understand the point of entering into the leadership coaching arena when there were so many amazing female coaches with massive followings and huge businesses already in place. Andrea questioned who would choose her as a coach over a *New York Times* bestselling author who was featured on every platform.

She started to question everything. Should she be a coach? Is the market oversaturated? Is there space for her voice amid all the competition already online? Eventually, she stopped creating inspirational content because she couldn't drown out the loud voice in her head saying, "Stop! You're wasting your time. Why can't you just be happy with the way things are? Why are you setting yourself up for the failure that awaits you?"

So, Andrea stopped working toward her dream of being a leadership coach and high-tailed it back to her comfort zone.

What Andrea didn't know yet, but I understood from past personal experience, is that just because you give up does not mean your inner calling will just shut up and go away. Oh no, it will only get louder and stronger (insert loud cackle from the Universe).

For the next few months, Andrea felt an overwhelming sense of disappointment that she had given up so quickly. I recommended that she find stories and books written by female coaches and entrepreneurs that share how they achieved success. She did, and do you know what she found out? Andrea discovered that *all* of them struggled with the catastrophic effects of comparison. The only difference was they didn't throw in the towel. Instead, they kept putting one foot in front of the other. Well, damn.

While it took several years to get Andrea back to the starting line of building her coaching practice, she got there. But this time, she was prepared, armed with the know-how to protect herself from the big, bad Comparison Monster.

Let us all learn from Andrea's experience—a little awareness and preparation can set you up to prevail over the inevitable tendency to compare yourself, your life, and your progress to that of others.

COMPARISON IS A LOSING GAME

The first step is always self-awareness. You need to understand the poisonous effects of comparison.

Comparison isn't complicated. It's our need to assign value to ourselves relative to others, either directed *up* or *down*. In an *upward comparison,* your subject is someone you perceive to have achieved more or to be better than you. The resulting thought is generally something like, "I'll never achieve what they've achieved," or, "They are far more talented than me."

A downward comparison is at play when you look at others and think, "Well, at least I'm doing better than they are." This gives you a sense of superiority and boosts your ego, knowing you are ahead. Even if you are just one person ahead, at least you are not *last*!

Whether you're focusing up or down, comparison is negative emotional hygiene and not productive. Why do we need to justify who we are, what we are doing, and where we are on our journey by measuring ourselves against others?

I need you to hear this: Someone else's success, or lack thereof, has absolutely nothing to do with you.

We are programmed to believe there is only *one* winner in the game of life. If someone has already won, they have taken what's yours, and you are relegated to the sidelines for eternity. There is only one first place, right? This way of thinking comes about mainly because comparison and competition are close cousins.

Competition has existed since the beginning of time. Even though it has some positive effects like motivating us to work harder and achieve our goals, its root is in scarcity. Ultimately, the idea of a limited supply of success is a good coverup for insecurities and the need to prove self-worth. After all, if you are the winner, no one can say you are not qualified or good enough. You have the Super Bowl ring to prove it!

This is not to say that only men do this, as women find ways to compare and compete creatively—children's grades, job titles, vacation plans, waist size, cooking ability, social calendar, housekeeping perfection, and so on. We have all grown up with these outdated modes of one-upmanship, driven by ideas of "eat or be eaten" and "get what's yours at any cost." But it doesn't have to be this way. What if we can all be winners in our own lives? What if there's enough room in the Universe for us to all be victorious in fulfilling our purpose?

One idea that helped me and acted as a comfort blanket in moments of doubt is: *What's yours will not be withheld from you. Your destiny is chasing you just as much as you are pursuing it.* When you see someone else shining and experiencing success, that is *theirs* to experience. It is meant for them. Your success is meant for you. You didn't miss an opportunity or lose your shot just because someone else got the job or landed a hot date.

If you lose the job, it's not yours anymore. If you didn't get the callback for the audition, the part wasn't meant for you. But it also wasn't a mistake for you to go for it. Ask yourself what you learned from the experience. A guarantee: The experience of trying and not getting what you *think* should be yours is just as valuable as getting it.

Every moment is preparing you for what is to come. And you are always right on time!

Your journey to fulfilling your destiny might take twice as long, or it could be twice as fast; it might zig and zag while others go straight, and it might require ten steps or one thousand. Just because your path to success looks different from others doesn't make it wrong. It is yours, and it is designed *for* you.

The worst thing you can do is compare your beginning to someone's middle or end. You are at the beginning of something amazing. Don't let someone else's progress demoralize you.

Let's look at ways you can handle the urge to measure yourself against others when comparison rears its ugly head.

HOW TO SHIFT OUT OF COMPARISON

Identify your triggers

One of my favorite quotes, often attributed to Socrates, is "Know thyself." We could jam on that profound quote for an entire book, but you have to get real with your triggers right now. Until you can release the thoughts that cause negative emotions when you see someone else experiencing the success you desire and doing the work you dream of doing, stop seeking them out.

I took a social media detox for this very reason. I noticed that I felt deflated and anxious after scrolling through Instagram, so I stopped.

If you got excruciating stomach cramps every time you ate ice cream, I bet you would lay off the dairy, right? We must take the same precautions with our mental and emotional health as with our physical body.

Now, grab a pen and paper and jot down when and where you find yourself engaging in negative comparison. What are the repetitive thoughts you experience? Who is with you? What are you doing?

This inquiry is not about blaming yourself or feeling shame for allowing others to make you feel crappy. It's about giving yourself a break from those actions to heal. What worked for Andrea was taking a break from surfing the web and actively looking for other successful coaches. For you, it might require spending less time with a particular friend or unfollowing certain people on Instagram. At least for a while, honor what you need and love yourself enough to take action to eliminate the triggering activities and people.

Celebrate your strengths

No human can ever be directly compared to another because we are all so damn different! There will never be an apples-to-apples scenario here. I challenge you to find another human who looks identical to you (identical twins excluded). I challenge you to find another human who has had the same experiences you have had, including thinking the same thoughts about those experiences. I challenge you to find someone with the same skill set, gifts, and interests.

You have a unique perspective to offer. There is no other you. You are a one-of-a-kind limited edition just the way you are. You are *irreplaceable*!

I love to write and have set a goal to write and publish fifty books in my lifetime. Do you know how many other books have been, and will be, written on the same topics I will write about? Millions, but none of them will be like mine because they won't be written from my perspective. So, why should I think there's no room for my contribution?

What do you do well? What skills and strengths do you have within you to bring forth your purpose and mission? It is time to celebrate and feel proud of all of those strengths and skills you've honed by being you, living your life, and experiencing the world as only you can.

Have a little talk with yourself

When was the last time you gave yourself a time-out?

When my children were being completely ridiculous and misbehaving, a good ole' five-minute time out was enough to sort them out. When you are in a whirlwind of negative mind-chatter about why you're not good enough or as good as so-and-so, find a quiet place to relax and chat with yourself.

My chats sound like this: "Hey you, you're doing great right where you are. Look at how far you've come. The Anniston of five years ago would be proud of where you are now. Stop looking at what everyone else is doing and refocus on *your* path. No one can fulfill your destiny except you. Let's f'ing go."

And when I feel better, I excuse myself from time-out. Taking a quick solo stroll around the neighborhood is also effective if you are averse to sitting in a chair in the corner.

Focus on your wins

American attorney and senator Dan Sullivan, in his book *The Gap and the Gain*, explains that we all have an elusive ideal target that is out of reach. If we continue to measure ourselves against that target, we are in the gap. However, if we can measure ourselves backward against our previous selves instead, we are in the *gain.*

If you commit to ending your week by focusing on the *gains,* you will start to feel better. You will also begin to feel the momentum of forward movement speeding up as what you focus on expands.

Learn to compete with yourself

Competition is only valuable when you are competing against yourself. One sport I adore is rock climbing. I started in my early twenties, and while I don't have as much time for it now, I still miss the meditative quality of climbing. When you are midway through a route, it is just you and the rock face. It's about keeping fear at bay, focusing on the next move, and looking for efficiencies and ways to improve your form to conserve energy and move effectively. Your focus is on *you* because that is where your power is. If you were to stop climbing and look around to see what other climbers around you are doing, you would lose strength, focus, and the ability to hold on to the rock.

Nobody else can fulfill your destiny, so stay focused on your path and aim to get better, bit by bit, every day.

Give to others what you want for yourself

If you find yourself in a fit of comparison, the quickest exit route is to focus outward. How can you give someone else what you want? How can you celebrate the wins of others just the way you would like others to do for you? How can you *help* others achieve greatness?

Everything you want is inside you: love, freedom, abundance, security, and joy. When you intentionally give others what you seek, it also activates the same within you. Your soul knows this, and it pisses your ego off. Lean into your generosity. It's the secret sauce.

Find an expander

Rather than looking for others to compare yourself to, why don't you actively look for others who can *expand* your belief about what is possible? I believe Jesus Christ is an old-school *expander*, showing the world what is possible when you choose love over fear and know you are connected to everyone and everything.

Who can you identify as an expander in your life right now? Who represents what you want to be, do, and achieve? Let that individual be a beacon of possibility for you. Let their success bolster your confidence in doing the same. Allow your belief about what is possible to be challenged and stretched every time you see them in their greatness.

Comparison is just a symptom of a lack of self-worth and self-love, and it's a horrible way to spend your energy. When you accept yourself fully and know yourself to be a one-of-a-kind, creative being who has a unique path to follow to your destiny, there is no need to do anything but celebrate and encourage others on their journeys.

When you can positively observe the gifts and achievements of others, you will be able to see and celebrate your own.

Let those farther along on their journey show you the way while you turn back and do the same for those behind you. This is the way, one hand reaching forward and the other reaching back.

PUTTING IT INTO PRACTICE

Identify five expanders in your life; if you don't have any, it's time to start looking.

Select individuals who exhibit qualities you would like to possess and have achieved the success you seek. You might not find one person with every quality, but that's okay. You can collect expanders who demonstrate different qualities, skills, and achievements.

Write them down in your journal. Follow them on social media. Surround yourself with people who have achieved greatness, and you will be reminded of what is possible.

Part 3

FOLLOW THE ROADMAP

Chapter 9

START WHERE YOU ARE

Start from wherever you are, with whatever you've got.

—Jim Rohn, American Entrepreneur and Author

THIS CHAPTER IS THE BEGINNING of the road map—the starting point. There's only so much time you can spend preparing. Eventually, you have to start *being* the person you've defined in your new vision.

I was thirty-one when I received my first book idea. I remember waking up from a dream in which some nameless person told me about this book I was to write, and in the dream, I kept thinking: *Write a book? There's no way.* Over the following days, I couldn't stop thinking about that dream and the unbelievable storyline I had been given. At that point, I hadn't defined my purpose and wasn't aware that writing would be a part of it. Mostly because I had never seriously considered writing anything and certainly hadn't tried. I was comfortable *consuming* books, but *creating* them was another story.

I told Rudi about the dream, and he responded, "Anniston, why don't you at least try to write it? What do you have to lose?" In my heart, I knew he was right, but I also couldn't ignore the repetitive thought that I wasn't capable of writing anything worth reading. Yet, something deep inside was urging me forward, and it scared the hell out of me.

So, I did what most do in this fearful state: I busied myself *preparing* to write. I read books on writing fiction, watched tutorials online, and listened to podcasts where authors talked about this elusive craft. Then, I figured I needed to create a "writing space" in our house. I cleared out a spare bedroom, painted it bright purple (don't ask me why), arranged and rearranged the furniture, and set up my desk.

I was finally ready to begin. I blocked off time on my calendar to write, and when it finally came time to peer into that blank Word document on my laptop, I was overwhelmed. Every sentence I wrote felt childish, clunky, and forced. I couldn't figure out how to start this book, overanalyzing every word and retyping the same paragraph multiple times. I spent six hours sitting at my writing desk that day only to delete every word I'd written by the end.

As the sun set that evening, I felt frustrated and disempowered. If this was something I was *supposed* to do, it should've come easily and felt natural. I poured myself a generous glass of wine and grabbed some of my favorite novels off the bookshelf to see how those writers had begun their books. Page after page, I read beautiful, compelling words that seemed to flow perfectly from one to the next. How could I ever *compare* to that? They were real writers—I was just a woman who had a dream but wasn't qualified to write anything. This wine-filled crisis of confidence validated my desire to never return to my writing desk. And I didn't for *three years*.

Now you understand why I made you endure the previous super-fun chapters on managing your fears, limiting beliefs, imposter syndrome, and comparison. They are your biggest obstacles to getting started and will often stop you *before* you even set out.

Here's the thing: You're *never* going to feel ready to do something you've never done or to be someone you've never been. You can spend a lifetime planning, organizing, brainstorming, and strategizing. But *experience* is always the best teacher, and it's the only way you will gain the confidence to move forward.

The reason I recommend for people to "start where you are" rather than "start once you've quit your current job" is that we often think we need to leave the job we're in to become who we want to be. But what happens when you're a year into your next job and start to feel those same feelings of dissatisfaction and unfulfillment? Are you going to leave that job, too? And what kind of pressure and stress are you putting on yourself financially during that time?

Alternatively, you can start being who you want to be *now* and see where that takes you. You can keep earning that paycheck while stretching into this new life you are creating for yourself. It might lead to leaving your job for another, but it's also possible that the opportunity to share your gifts and purpose exists right where you are.

One of my coaching clients, Carol, was a successful woman in her sixties who had made millions but felt unfulfilled and lost. She was considering resigning from her current seven-figure job in sales to pursue her dream of being an inspirational speaker, inspiring single moms to take their power back and create wealth. During one of our first calls, she asked, "What must I do to fulfill this dream? Quit my job?"

I said, "Possibly—but before you jump to that conclusion, let's start with your dream of being an inspirational speaker and teacher. Where in your life are you doing that now?" She explained that she was active in her church and volunteered at a women's shelter a few times a week, where she would offer counsel to women in need. I said, "Great! How about at work?"

She paused and said, "Well, that's not something I do at work, and it's certainly not part of my job function." She then shared her concerns that her coworkers would judge her or that her superiors would think she had gone crazy and she would lose her job.

I gave her an assignment. For the next month, she was to find any opportunity at work to inspire, motivate, and uplift the people around her. I encouraged her to show up as an inspirational speaker and teacher in her *current* role.

On our next call, Carol showed up bubbling with excitement to share her experience. She explained that it felt awkward and incredibly vulnerable to instigate personal conversations with her colleagues at first. However, her nervousness quickly subsided when she experienced their response. She realized women and men around her were in pain—quietly dealing with past traumas, anxiety, and depression. She started connecting with her colleagues and clients on a much deeper level because she was brave enough to ask real questions like, "What can I do to support you?" and "How are you feeling these days?"

Encouraged by her coworkers' receptiveness, Carol soon felt courageous enough to share her own story of being a single mother, struggling to put food on the table, and fighting depression and suicidal thoughts before she reached out for help and did the work to turn her life around. She then felt inspired to invite all the women in her department to an after-hours get-together where they could share their stories and receive inspiration and support. A woman from the HR department joined and approached Carol afterward to ask if she would be willing to speak at the upcoming company conference.

Carol was finally getting her opportunity to be an inspirational speaker on the big stage. But little did she know that her first audience would be those she had worked with for decades.

You guys, this all occurred in *four* weeks. She went from *wanting* to be an inspirational teacher and speaker to *being* one, and miracles started to happen and continued to do so.

As we already discussed at the beginning of the book, you are where you are for a reason. Maybe it's so you can get clarity on what you *don't* want so you'll be able to better create what you do, or perhaps it's because you're meant to serve the people around you. We often don't understand how life's experiences serve us until we look back.

I must reemphasize that expressing your purpose may or may not be tied to your paycheck. And that's okay—it doesn't make it any more or less valuable. The value comes in the impact you make in the world and, more importantly, the fulfillment and joy you feel. It's equally vital for you to get started right where you are.

The most powerful action you can take to move your life forward is to start embodying what you want to be *right now*, regardless of your current job title and function. If you want to be a chef, I bet there are hungry people in your office who would love to try your creations. If you want to be an artist, start creating thank you cards and sending them to your coworkers and clients. If you want to be a homeowner, start putting away money for a down payment. If you want to be an author, set your alarm for 5 a.m. and dedicate the first hour of your day to writing your first book.

Like anything else, you need to understand the benefits of this approach to willingly take the uncomfortable action.

NOW IS THE NEW LATER

One of my favorite books is *The Power of Now* by Eckhart Tolle. In this groundbreaking book, Tolle teaches that the *present* is all you have. Time is an illusion, and when you focus on what is happening *now*, you can experience true peace and radically transform your life.

It makes sense if you think about it. When you're imagining a future, you're always focusing on a point in time where you are *not*. There is a built-in separation between where you are and where you want to be, and that separation can cause a lot of pain and suffering. While spending time visualizing and planning your future is essential, your power to create that future is in this moment, which is wherever you are reading these words.

If you believed that taking one action toward your dream right now would redirect the trajectory of your life toward your desired outcome, *would you do it?* Alternatively, would you wait if you knew that delaying to start till tomorrow would keep your future the same as your past?

You can't *wait* and *create* simultaneously—it's one or the other.

An incredibly talented colleague of mine had an idea to create a new department in our company that would allow us to attract and serve high-spend clients. She told me about her vision and said she was working on a proposal to present to the senior vice president. I assumed this would take her a few months to get off the ground. To my surprise, within a few *weeks,* she had finished her proposal, pitched it, and was being promoted and given a budget to hire a team for her new department—weeks, not months.

The Universe rewards speed. Don't put off doing something today that could change your tomorrow.

PUT YOUR STAKE IN THE SAND

When you start taking action, others pay attention. I would bet that the people close to you are pretty familiar with your current personality—how you act, talk, and behave. They *know* you—or at least the character you've presented to them. So, what happens when you want to change?

If you're just *talking* about what you want to do, create, or be, they likely won't believe you (even if they pretend to). Some will hope you *don't* change because they unconsciously need you to stay the same so they know what to expect from you, which makes them feel comfortable. Remember, the unknown can feel scary—especially if you fear a loved one might leave or do something crazy and lose everything.

My philosophy is simple: Don't tell them, *show them.* When you take action, you're telling yourself and the people around you that you're not playing around. You're demonstrating your desire through taking courageous steps forward, and you're not asking for their permission or approval to do so. Warning: This will be very triggering for some of your loved ones. They might even give you their unsolicited opinions and advice, and to that, all you have to do is say, "Thank you for your concern; I'll take that into consideration."

In my experience, putting a stake in the sand in the form of action ignites a universal ripple effect of synchronicities, unexpected support, and opportunities coming out of nowhere. It's almost as if the Universe is waiting to see if you're serious. I imagine spiritual beings watching me take big, bold action, then sounding a trumpet announcing, "Okay guys, better get to work. She's not messing around!"

YOU MAKE A DECISION

One of the worst things you can do is be indecisive about moving forward. *Should I? Shouldn't I? Will I? Won't I?* The longer you stay in that place, the more you are in danger of giving up on living and expressing your highest self. It's also exhausting, as all your energy is directed toward making a decision versus using that precious energy to take action.

You need to check in with yourself to determine if your trepidation comes from your inner guidance system saying, "Don't do this," or from self-created, unconscious fears. I have *not* taken action when it didn't feel right, and I've been happy for it when I realized it wasn't the best move forward or the proper time. However, most of the time, you'll find the reason you aren't moving forward is that you're paralyzed by fear of failure, success, judgment, or rejection.

What if you couldn't make a mistake? Think about it for a second—taking action will result in experience. After taking every action, you'll gain clarity and see things from a slightly different lens. If a decision leads to an outcome you don't like, that's feedback. You can now choose differently based on what you've just learned. When you know better, you *do* better.

You have nothing to lose and everything to learn.

YOU GAIN CONFIDENCE

I can't tell you how many times I've heard from coaching clients, colleagues, and friends that confidence is what they feel they lack the most in life. They say, "How can I get more confidence to pursue my dreams? How can I feel more confident in my talents and abilities?"

Courage comes before confidence. First, you need to muster the courage to try something new. Then, you need to practice and gain experience. The more you practice, the more competent you will feel, and competence breeds confidence.

Over a decade ago, Rudi and I decided to dedicate our lives to helping others through coaching and spiritual mentorship. However, we didn't know where to start. We built a website and started posting online, but nothing was happening. We desperately wanted this to work but had no idea how to get this coaching business off the ground.

One day, I got the idea to start a meetup group at our house to offer coaching support for those in need. My plan was for us to post the event using the Meetup online platform and see if anyone showed up. When I told Rudi about this, he thought I was crazy. "You want to invite strangers into our home, people who don't know anything about us, for us to coach for free?" That was a fun debate, which I eventually won.

Only *two* people showed up for the first meetup. We were so nervous and awkward, but we dove in and gave them each time to share a problem, situation, or question and receive coaching and feedback. This first meetup was scary, but after it was over, we were glowing with excitement. We had spent two hours *coaching,* and it felt damn good. Five people came to the second meetup, and eight showed up for the third. Word started to spread, and the attendees continued to bring their friends and family. Eventually, up to fifty people gathered in our little living room. We did this for *three years*, hosting over fifty live group coaching sessions before saying goodbye as we moved out of state and on to the next chapter.

The meetups became our coaching practice field, and our nervousness was replaced by confidence week by week. We learned so much about people's needs, their most significant obstacles, and how to support them best to move forward. We never charged a dime for these meetups—our reward was confidence. Not only did we know we could make an impact on people, but we had no doubt it was part of our destiny to do so.

Confidence comes from within, but it doesn't come for free—it's *earned* by taking consistent action and gaining experience.

YOU GAIN SUPPORT

When you start taking action toward a goal, you put yourself in a position of being seen and noticed by like-minded people interested in working with and supporting you.

When you stop thinking about doing something and start doing it, you're going to put yourself in spaces and places with others who might need the very product or services you offer. Also, you're going to find that those who have successfully done what you're seeking to do will often turn around and excitedly teach others. As Jim Rohn says, "Success leaves clues."

The benefits of starting on your journey to aligning with and expressing your authentic purpose far outweigh any thoughts of waiting till tomorrow, next week, next month, or next year.

You are ready right now, just as you are. When you start *being* what you seek to be and doing what this version of you would be doing, it ceases to be a matter of if it will happen and becomes a matter of when.

I want to share some advice to support you in getting started—the ideas and tools that were super impactful on my journey to living my purpose.

START *BEING* WHO YOU WANT TO BE

Ask yourself the following questions:

- How can I show up today as my future self?
- What qualities do I need to develop?
- How can I start *being* what I want to be?

Do you need to be bolder and more courageous to achieve your goals? If so, set a goal to take one brave action today.

Do you want to feel more like an artist? Set aside an hour today to start your next art project.

Do you want to be the vice president of your organization? Schedule a thirty-minute meeting with your boss to ask for feedback on what you can work on to be considered for a promotion.

One of the quickest ways to start being who you want to be is to actively look for opportunities to insert your authentic self, talents, and abilities.

Rudi's client roster started expanding when he showed up as a coach *everywhere*—not just on his coaching calls and onstage. Whether in line at the grocery store, standing at the grill at a neighborhood barbeque, or sitting in a boardroom full of executives, he showed up as a *coach.* People started to notice, and because they could feel his authenticity, they would often ask for his business card. Rudi met one of his most recent clients seated next to him on a two-hour flight. When the man learned Rudi was a coach, he asked for his advice. Rudi's willingness to support him with a problem he was having landed him a lucrative client who genuinely values his services.

- Start *being* an artist by creating time every day to create art.
- Start being an influential teacher by creating an online course.
- Start being a loving mother by volunteering at a local community center that provides childcare for single mothers in need.
- Start *being* a bestselling author by joining a writer's group and asking for feedback on your manuscript.
- Start *being* a comedian by writing one new joke a day and sharing it with your colleagues over lunch.
- Start *being* a healthy, fit individual by studying nutrition and eating the way you imagine your future healthy self would eat.

Anytime you're expanding into a higher version of yourself, it will feel like you're wearing someone else's clothes that don't fit quite right. You've got to grow into your new self, and the easiest way to do that is to spend time doing the things that will allow you to believe you already are who you want to be.

LET GO OF THE OUTCOME

It's natural to imagine what outcome each action will bring and then to feel disappointed if that doesn't happen. My advice is to remain *unattached* to the outcome of each of your actions.

You will never fully comprehend the impact of your actions, mainly because you'll experience the beautiful compound effect in the form of forward movement as you continue down this path. For instance, you could post for three hundred days straight and get a direct message from someone asking for your services on post number three hundred and one.

As opportunities come your way, your job is to say *yes,* as long as it feels aligned with your purpose, and to trust that it's serving a purpose. This is the approach I choose to take, and that's all I need to know. The outcome is not up to me, nor is it my business. I look at each opportunity to show up as my authentic self and express my purpose as a *divine assignment.*

Letting go of the outcome allows you to relax into the journey, creating space for synchronicities and miracles to flow to you and through you.

BREAK YOUR BIG GOAL DOWN INTO SMALL STEPS

One of my favorite quotes, often attributed to Martin Luther King, Jr., is "Take the first step in faith. You don't have to see the whole staircase, just take the first step."

It's a good idea to take another look at the new vision you created for yourself. Who do you need to *be,* and what do you need to *do*? Write it out and get clear. Then, break down those goals into small, manageable daily steps. If you allow yourself to focus on *all* the steps required, it will feel too big, and your fears and limiting beliefs will get the better of you.

Get in the practice of declaring the action you will take, no matter how small, and then commit to completing it. This daily practice will move you forward quickly and help you develop trust in your ability to do what you say you're going to do. You'll also get a daily dopamine hit when you celebrate reaching your daily action goal.

PUTTING IT INTO PRACTICE

Pick one of your big goals defined in your new vision. Grab a journal and answer the following questions.

1. What action am I committed to achieving today, and how will I feel when I reach it?
2. What qualities can I express today that will support my new vision?

Are you ready to start the most exciting journey of your life? *Starting right where you are* is the first step to living a life of fulfillment, joy, and success beyond your wildest imagination.

Better buckle up—your train is leaving the station.

Chapter 10

TAKE INSPIR-ACTION

When the basis for your actions is inner alignment
with the present moment, your actions become
empowered by the intelligence of life itself.

—Eckhart Tolle

IT WAS THE FALL OF 2020, and while the world was still in the throes of COVID-19 and I was furloughed from my corporate job, our coaching business was thriving.

I had just come off the high of hosting and producing an online interview series, which was exhilarating and highly successful. This initiative required much time and effort, so I was equally ready to celebrate and sleep! I knew I needed a break before diving back into our business. So, I took a week to recalibrate and enjoy every second of sleeping in, reading books, and taking boat rides with Rudi and the kids.

On day eight, I was ready to return to work. Rudi was spending most of his time leading the coaching calls and pouring into our clients, so I was tasked with business development and expanding our audience.

I was well-versed in business practices, having worked in sales and advertising for two decades. I knew everything we *should* be doing to build our business; however, none of those tasks felt exciting at the time. I could create an email campaign, social media strategy, lead-in offers, media exposure opportunities, you name it. The list of actions to take in building a business is endless. But right then, they all felt like *work.*

I would love to tell you I closed my laptop and extended my vacation, but I didn't. I did what I thought was the next best step: I created an online coaching program and a campaign to support its launch. Again, this massive project required tremendous planning, scripting, filming, and post-production work for Rudi and me. But, unlike the previous project for which I had endless creative energy and motivation, this one felt tedious and laborious. I felt stressed and anxious about completing and launching the program by my deadline. Still, I pushed through because we had already promoted the launch date. There was no going back—I was committed.

We created a solid, transformational online course in less than six weeks. The launch was upon us, and we had done *everything* to ensure great success. Yet I had an uneasy feeling in my gut, a weird sensation that something was *off*—a feeling I had carried from the start.

The launch date arrived, and we had an excellent turnout for the promotional event we had planned. The audience was receptive and excited to hear all the details. As the call requests rolled in, we were confident we would fill the program without a problem. Unfortunately, that was not the case. Instead, it was a case of *failure to launch.*

On our calls, we heard comments like: "The program looks awesome, but it's just not the right time for me." "Wow, what a powerful program; let me think about it." "It's awesome, but it doesn't feel right for me right now."

We had put in *so* many hours, days, and weeks to create this program, resulting in just two enrollments that day. To say we felt deflated would be a massive understatement. Since launching our coaching business, this was the first time we felt the horrible sting of failure. Until then, success had come so easily. I was worried this setback was indicative of what was to come. Maybe we weren't on the right path? Maybe our dream of building a successful coaching company was unrealistic?

Rudi shook it off quickly and jumped back into serving our existing clients, but I did not. This failure rattled my confidence. I tried to figure out where we had gone wrong. What was so different about this project versus the successful ones that had come before it? Did the content fail to resonate? Was the value not there?

After days of reflection, I realized the result had nothing to do with the content. The program was excellent. The problem was rooted in how it began. The course wasn't something I *wanted* to do—it was something I thought we *should* do.

While this distinction might seem trivial, the difference in energy is monumental. In the past, when I had been inspired to do something, it felt like it was coming straight from the heart. I had done it even though it was not what I had been *thinking* the next step should be.

In contrast, this course had originated from the mind. I had to force myself to show up and push the project forward every day, and it put a massive strain on my physical, emotional, and mental health. Energetically, it sucked the life out of me.

To restate this simply: The idea for our online interview series came from *within,* while the idea for the online course came from *without.*

This was a "holy shit" mind-blowing revelation for me. I had just experienced the result of thinking my way forward instead of following my heart. This lesson was time-consuming and costly, yet incredibly valuable. I knew I needed to adopt a new approach to developing our business—and I was open to receiving some guidance on what that was.

While journaling one morning, I wrote the question: *What should I do to find clarity and direction for my next step?* I put on some music, sat down with pen and paper, and began automatic writing, allowing words to flow mindlessly from pen to page.

Later, when I reviewed what I had written, I saw the following sentences: *You should do a 30-day inspir-action challenge. It's time to reconnect to your higher self and receive daily guidance. Taking these inspired actions will lead to the clarity you desire.*

When I first read "inspir-action," I thought I'd made a spelling error and that it was meant to read "inspiration." But, as I began to edit, I had an inner knowing it was not an error but a great truth.

My soul was urging me to hone my ability to receive inspired ideas, trust the guidance, and take action. *Inspir-action.* The message came with a jolt of energy and made sense, so I accepted the challenge. It felt good to have a clear plan, even though I had no idea what it would lead to.

After meditating the following day, I eagerly grabbed my journal. As instructed, I wrote the question: *What action should I take today for my highest and greatest good?* I took a few deep breaths, clearing my mind in anticipation of receiving a revolutionary message. The words I received were*: Take a long walk on the beach.*

Not what I was expecting, but at least it was an enjoyable activity. I walked on the beach for over an hour that day. It was rejuvenating and enjoyable despite the voice in my head chastising me for having fun instead of moving our business forward.

The next day, I followed the same morning routine, and the words came: *Work in the garden.* I giggled, thinking that maybe my higher self wasn't interested in making money and wanted to simply have fun instead! Even so, I followed directions. I had forgotten how great it felt to spend time in our garden, pulling weeds and tending to our plants.

The following day, I was guided to spend time playing with my kids, and the next, to read and spend time in silence, and the next, to organize my closet. After a week of receiving guidance unrelated to our business, I felt frustrated and confused. The thought came to me: *If you need clarification, ask for clarity.*

In my journal, I posed the question: *Why do I keep receiving messages to do all of these unimportant tasks and activities instead of working on our business?* The answer came quickly: *You are a human being, not a human doing. Your energy is depleted; thus, you must take time to fill your cup and heal. These activities are for your business, and the ripple effects of feeling relaxed, rested, and rejuvenated are far greater than you will ever know.*

When truth finds you, you feel it, and these revelations landed for me in a big way. It is all connected: How we feel in our bodies, the health of our relationships, and our emotional state extends into every area of our lives, including our careers.

On day seven of the challenge, I received an assignment that pushed every one of my internal triggers. The inspiration I received was to *start an intention group . . . today!* I was to create an invite and send it out to our entire email list, promoting an opportunity to join a weekly call that I would facilitate—free of charge.

My mind was running a million miles a minute. This felt *way* too fast, and I certainly didn't have anything figured out. I kept thinking of why this would fail and argued with that internal voice that I needed much more time to pull this off. Yet, the guidance came with such a strong wave of inspiration and motivation that I couldn't stop thinking about it. Eventually, I said, "To hell with it," and started writing the email. One hour later—I hit send. A horrible vulnerability hangover quickly replaced the excitement. *Holy shit. What did I do?*

I follow the work of Lynne McTaggart, author of *The Intention Experiment* and *The Power of Eight*, who rigorously studies the science behind group intention. When a group of individuals hold the same intention simultaneously, the power of manifestation is amplified in miraculous ways for the sender and receiver. Still, I never imagined facilitating one of these groups.

How would people receive my email? Would they think I was crazy? Would they unsubscribe from the list? Would *anyone* come?

A week later, it was time for our first call. I logged on to Zoom and took a few minutes to quiet my mind. When I opened my eyes, there were over thirty people in the waiting room. To say I was pleasantly surprised (and totally freaked out) is an understatement.

That day, the InPowered Intention Group was created. Rudi joined in as co-host, and we both felt a strong connection with the participants as if we had all known one another for a long time. We looked forward to hosting these calls every two weeks, and the group started to grow naturally. We received the gift of witnessing large and small miracles occurring in the participants' lives over the next year. Members kept telling us how the community was a blessing and how they felt loved, accepted, and safe to be themselves. Over the next eighteen months, the Intention Group evolved, and the members came to the call requesting coaching and support. This group has now evolved into our InPowered Life community—a place for people to grow and elevate their lives together.

What started as an Intention Group has become one of our most outstanding achievements—the opportunity to generously give our love and time in exchange for the beautiful connections we have made and facilitated for others. It has changed many lives, and for us it has been a catalyst for many new clients, partnerships, and opportunities. It is the gift that keeps on giving.

My new standard operating procedure for our business is this way of being: receiving direction from within and following through by taking action.

While often scary, the guidance pushes me into unknown territory. It elevates my awareness of the power of aligning with my purpose and sharing my gifts with the world. The *things* that come from following my guidance have a high-vibe, expansive quality. They continue to grow and evolve; without exception, they serve my highest good and the highest good of others.

WHAT IS INSPIR-ACTION?

I like to describe "inspir-action" as the narrow strait between inspiration and action. It's the middle ground between yin and yang, left brain and right brain. Inspiration is inherently a yin, feminine quality received intuitively. Action is a yang, masculine quality.

I have worked with many powerful spiritual healers and teachers who embody feminine qualities in a yin way. They are intuitive, receptive, nurturing, and loving. They receive incredibly inspired ideas. Yet, when it comes to committing to take action, they struggle and often give up because they can't seem to create momentum.

On the other hand, I have observed men and women who are the *doers* of this world. These manifesting machines are constantly taking action toward their goals. However, what they create often leaves them feeling unsatisfied and wanting more. They are acting on what they *think* they should do instead of what they *feel* they should do.

You will need to align both with your purpose and the highest vision for your life. You have to find the balance between the feminine *receiving* and the masculine *doing.*

CREATE SPACE TO RECEIVE GUIDANCE

Have you ever noticed that you get great ideas while doing particular activities? One of my friends claims all her greatest inspirations have come while showering. For Rudi, taking a long walk or sitting in our sauna gets the ideas flowing. I receive lightning-strike ideas right after meditating or while reading a book. Both of those activities quiet my mind, and when I least expect it, the thought, answer, or solution to a problem will land in my awareness.

I recommend you intentionally create the space in your life to receive guidance from your higher self. We live in a noisy world, and our constant mind chatter is the loudest. Your soul is like the wise, calm, quiet friend you must strain to hear in a noisy restaurant. You have to listen with intent to hear its wise words.

Try setting a ten-to-fifteen-minute daily date with your higher self. Treat it like a morning meeting with your internal board of directors, a check-in to inquire about essential issues and formulate an action plan. If you had a daily meeting scheduled with your superiors at your job, would you miss it? No, because it is crucial to level-set and align on your daily tasks. It should be the same with your soul.

WHAT DOES INSPIRED GUIDANCE FEEL LIKE?

How do you know if the guidance you receive is from your ego or your soul? I dedicate an entire chapter to this in Part 3 of this book, but for now, know that your inner guidance comes from *feeling.*

Inspired ideas are often accompanied by a surge of energy and positive physical sensations in the body, such as goosebumps or full-body tingles.

You have to learn what a yes versus a no feels like by learning the language of your inner feelings. Your body will generally contract in your chest or stomach when something is not right for you. But, when it is a yes, you will feel an expansion, excitement, peace, and natural motivation.

It does not mean you won't have nervous butterflies. The guidance will often scare the crap out of you. It's important to know the difference between excited-nervous and anxious-nervous.

As bestselling author Tim Ferriss says, "The most important actions are never comfortable."

Why? Because success doesn't exist inside of your comfort zone. When you follow the inner urges of your soul, it *will* point you on a collision path with your greatest fears.

RIDE THE WAVE

The experience of taking inspired action can be likened to surfing.

Imagine sitting on a surfboard bobbing up and down on a calm sea. You face the horizon, taking in the sunrise as you wait for the next set of waves to roll in. You sit and wait patiently, knowing that no amount of action on your part will make the perfect wave come sooner. You see a wave forming in the distance, building speed as it gracefully moves toward you. When you feel the gentle pull of the current, you turn your board around and start to paddle with strength and urgency. The instant you feel yourself perfectly positioned with the wave, you lift yourself to a standing position, letting the force of the ocean carry you until it breaks near the shore and the ride is over.

Taking inspired action is all about timing. Once the surge of the idea moves through you, the initial energy and power of that idea will start to decrease. I used to receive ideas after meditation and excitedly write them down in my journal, my mind blown at how brilliant and perfect the inspiration was. Then, I would get busy with my day and often put off revisiting the idea. If I let a full day or two pass without investing any energy in acting on the inspiration, I would have a hard time catching the same excitement I initially felt.

Your journal can become the graveyard of inspired ideas. The positive energy you receive with an inspired idea is a gift. If you can catch those waves, you can take quantum leaps forward in your life. It will help you move through fear and procrastination, and manifest quickly. The ride on the wave will be extended with committed action.

I love the spiritual philosophy that ideas have their own energetic life form and purpose. What if a higher power chooses the individual who will bring an idea into manifest form? If the individual doesn't rise to the occasion, all is not lost; it will just find another willing participant. So, when you receive a damn good idea, you better claim it!

In her bestselling book *Big Magic*, author and speaker Elizabeth Gilbert says that when we receive ideas from within, we must honor them and act upon them promptly. If you don't take action, inspiration will find its home with another human partner willing and able to birth it into physical form.

You always have free will. You get to choose where to focus your creative energy and effort. Ultimately, the decision is yours regarding commitment to an inspiration. If an idea lights you up and something deep inside is saying yes, I advise you to take action immediately.

Here's my process:

- I write out inspired ideas I receive in a special notebook reserved for the ideas I intend to create.
- I immediately unpack all the information from the initial download and create a loose action plan.

Here's an example: I was inspired to write this book during a meditation. Afterward, I grabbed my ideas notebook and wrote the book's title. The outline quickly followed. I spent the next twenty minutes fleshing out the outline with ideas for chapter topics and significant themes. This is what I like to call the inspired idea brain dump.

Some ideas can be developed quickly, requiring only one action for completion. For example, if you are inspired to call a potential client, you could open your calendar to block off time to make the call that day or immediately send a message to the client requesting a call.

If you are inspired to share a message on social media, don't overthink it, and don't get bogged down in perfectionism. Just do it! The longer you wait, the more likely it is that your mind will convince you of all the reasons it is a waste of time or not in your best interest.

If you are unsure what to do, ask your higher self, "What would it take for me to create this?" Ask for guidance, wait for the answer to come to you, and be prepared to receive.

If you are plagued with fear about taking action on an inspired idea, it is because you are making it about *you.* What if the concept you received will change the lives of everyone in the entire world? What if this idea will save even just one life? Would it be worth following the guidance and taking action?

Your calling comes from within, so it makes sense that the instructions to manifest your calling will also come from within, right? Every time you courageously follow the inspired ideas from your heart, you are stepping onto a path *no one else* has traveled. This is a great declaration to the Universe that you are not here to follow and imitate what has come before but to discover your own truth and create from that space.

Those who follow their inner calling, committing to action and picking up the breadcrumbs as they appear, are the great innovators and initiators that will birth a new world into form.

PUTTING IT INTO PRACTICE

If you genuinely want to experience a lifetime of fulfillment, joy, and success, you must learn to dance to the beat of your own drum. I recommend you create a practice of checking in for your daily assignments and trusting that guidance above anything else. This practice will *ensure* you stay on track with your purpose and destiny. It also comes with the added benefit of less stress, more fun, and quantum leaps toward successful outcomes.

For the next thirty days, I challenge you to spend ten to fifteen minutes each morning doing the following:

- Grab a notebook and pen and sit in a comfortable position.
- Take a few minutes to quiet your mind, taking deep breaths until your mind and body are calm.
- Put your hand over your heart and ask, "What aligned action can I take today?"
- Allow time for ideas to present themselves in your awareness. Even if they don't come right then, be open and present throughout the day, as you may receive them later.
- When you receive an idea, answer the following questions:
  - How would you describe your inspired idea?
  - How did it feel when you received it?
  - How could acting on this idea benefit your life or others?
  - What action could you take today toward creating this idea?

Chapter 11

GO ALL IN

The biggest commitment you must keep
is your commitment to yourself.
—Neale Donald Walsch, American Author,
Actor, Screenwriter, and Speaker

ONE DAY, I RECEIVED THE inspiration to create a podcast.

I had just finished meditating, and *bam*, the inspiration landed in my mind, beautifully wrapped and full of energy and excitement for what this could be. I grabbed my journal and took as many notes as possible while the inspiration was fresh in my mind.

I've always been an avid podcast consumer. I have a library of my favorites and love to take long walks while listening to insightful and inspiring conversations. To imagine that my husband Rudi and I could have our own podcast made my heart leap out of my chest.

I ran downstairs and told Rudi, "We're going to start a podcast!"

He raised his eyebrows and gave me a look that said, "Really? With all the other projects we have going on?"

To be fair, we had *a lot* going on. Rudi's calendar was chock-full of coaching clients and businesses he was supporting with weekly training. I was working full time, traveling a few times a month, assisting Rudi with creating content for a course, and, of course, taking care of two beautiful kids who were involved in lots of extracurricular activities.

Our plates were already stacked high; however, I knew what an inspired idea felt like, and *this was definitely it!* I assured him it wouldn't be that hard—I could figure out all the nuts and bolts, and I was sure that we could have it ready to go within a month, maybe less.

He shook his head in a way that translates to, *I don't agree, but I'm going to because I know you've already made up your mind*, and said, "Sure."

This was not a completely foreign idea. Rudi and I had spoken about starting a podcast many times—our friends and family had even suggested it because we *love* having deep, profound conversations together. We are both professional public speakers and have no problem freestyling into a microphone for hours. Questions like, "What's your purpose in life?" and "What action can you take now to achieve your goals?" are everyday dinner table conversations in our home. I knew this would be the perfect way to use our gifts to increase our reach and impact.

That day, I carved out some time to do initial research and found an online guide called *How to Start a Podcast in 30 Days.* It seemed easy enough, so I wrote out all the tasks and assigned deadlines.

The first few steps were simple and fun—create a name for the podcast, hire a designer to create the cover image, and order a proper microphone and headphones. Check, check, and check! I was on track with the plan, and it felt great. But then I came up against some tasks that didn't feel as easy, like scripting our show intro and narrowing down the content, creating a schedule of episodes, and inviting guest speakers.

These steps shouldn't have felt hard, but when doubt started to interfere, I procrastinated and got lost in a silly cycle of perfectionism. I must have written the show intro fifty times, changing one word for another, but none of them felt right. I made a list of episode titles but started to question whether they would be appealing to our audience and whether it was the right content altogether. I created a list of guests to invite on the show but then convinced myself I needed to delay reaching out because who would want to record an episode for a podcast that hadn't launched yet?

In hindsight, my triggers were popping off like fireworks. The reality of what a podcast would require was setting in, and it made me feel uneasy and exposed. We would have to show up and share our stories, secrets, beliefs, and opinions with complete strangers. It would require me to be completely vulnerable—no hiding or sugarcoating. And I would have *no control* over how it would be perceived. Yikes!

Rather than dealing with these fears, I avoided working on the podcast, running back to the tasks and projects that were totally within my comfort zone. And I made sure to stack my plate so full of unnecessary tasks that I felt completely justified in putting off the podcast endeavor. It didn't take long before it became a file sitting on my desktop—an incomplete project put on hold for a rainy day. And that's where it lived for over a year.

Then, while participating in an intense transformational leadership course, I was challenged to declare a stretch goal, something that would force me to reach far outside my comfort zone to complete. The stakes were at an all-time high, as I wouldn't graduate the course unless I achieved my declared goal within a ninety-day timeframe.

I had many ideas for what I could declare: complete the first draft of my book, get promoted to vice president, or even walk ten thousand steps a day for ninety days. All of those felt like great options . . . if I were going to play it safe. But I wasn't taking the course so I could grow incrementally; I was taking it so I could take massive leaps forward in every area of my life. Ultimately, I chose the goal that was going to force me to face my greatest fears and triggers: the *podcast*.

In my heart, I knew it would be the perfect vehicle to defeat my arch nemesis—the fear of being seen, vulnerable, rejected, and judged. I declared my goal of creating and launching our podcast, with twelve episodes to be uploaded in ninety days. There was no going back now—shit just got real. There were over 150 successful leaders in this course, and the idea of admitting to all of them that I didn't achieve my goal would be so humiliating. Come hell or high water, I was not going to let that happen.

I revisited the folder on my desktop titled "Podcast" and got to work. But this time, I needed a rock-solid achievement plan. I started by reverse engineering each task based on the deadline and knew I'd have to get moving in order to get it all done. We had a lot going on at the time, so it forced me to get creative with my time management; lots of early mornings and weekends were going to be reallocated to this project.

Not having the luxury of time meant I didn't have the luxury of being indecisive. There was no room for overthinking, adding in a bunch of unnecessary steps, and getting stuck in the details. I had to commit to progress, not perfectionism. And let me tell you, it was a *massive* relief.

Tasks that had taken me days or even weeks to complete before were now taking less than an hour. I was shocked to know I had the capability to work at this speed and still create a great product I could be proud of. I experienced such a sense of accomplishment after each episode was recorded, and it was *so* much fun. Rudi and I agreed there would be no episode scripts, just an authentic, free-flowing conversation. We didn't allow ourselves to go back and listen or to rerecord any episodes, trusting that our intention to create the most impactful, inspiring content for our listeners would be enough. Before I knew it, we had recorded, edited, and uploaded the twelfth episode—just three days before graduation from my leadership course.

I had remained faithful to my commitment, and now I had something absolutely amazing that would create a massive impact for years to come.

The leadership training and course content didn't create the change I wanted. It was the ninety-day journey, each and every step, to completing the podcast that *was* the vehicle for my transformation.

Here's what I learned:

- I had a negative pattern of becoming inspired to initiate something and then failing to complete it. This pattern had nothing to do with my ability or willpower and everything to do with the deep wounds and fears of judgment and rejection I had yet to address.
- My indecisiveness and procrastination were not fixed qualities but symptoms of my limiting beliefs standing in the way.

- When my focus is on completing a task to the best of my ability rather than on the outcome, I don't allow myself to get caught up in the horrible cycle of fear, doubt, and imposter syndrome.

And I became aware—with every fiber of my being—that with focus and pure commitment, there's absolutely *nothing* I can't achieve. If I continue to put one foot in front of the other, I will get there.

I decided it was time to forgive myself for all the commitments I had failed to honor and the perceived missed opportunities. When you know better, you do better. And it was time for me to create a new narrative: the story of a woman who is 100 percent committed to following the guidance of her heart like her life depends on it.

How many times have you started something and didn't follow it through to completion? How many website domain names have you bought that have gone unused? How many book outlines still sit on your computer waiting to be written? How many side businesses have you started and stopped midway through?

Now let me ask you this: Do you keep daily commitments to yourself? Do you keep your promise if you say you'll get up at 5 a.m. and meditate? If you commit to being home by 5 p.m. after work to play with your kids, do you show up at 5:30 p.m. instead?

If you don't keep commitments to yourself, I bet you have difficulty keeping promises to others. There's *power* in doing what you say you will when you say you will do it. That's a highly sought-after quality, not just in the world but within yourself.

Imagine what it would feel like if you knew without a shadow of a doubt that when you committed to doing something, you would 100 percent complete it. How confident would you be in taking on challenging tasks? How empowered would you be to leave situations that no longer felt aligned so you could head down a different road and create something new?

Commitment is a muscle you must flex, strengthen, and stretch—it will be the key to not just dreaming about living your purpose but actually manifesting it.

Fulfilling your destiny requires a deep, rock-solid, immovable commitment to yourself and to following the guidance of your heart. It's a lifetime commitment to following what feels *right* and to saying no to those things that don't.

To prepare to make the most important commitment of your life, you must start building upon the belief that the Universe is conspiring with you rather than against you. Just as in any relationship, you have to begin building trust.

THE TRUST GAME

Have you ever done a relationship-building activity at work where you are paired with someone and each of you takes turns falling backward, trusting that your partner (usually some random colleague from another department) will catch you?

Having worked in and out of Corporate America for many years, I've been a part of and have observed several of these "trust fall" sessions. While most people roll their eyes and look annoyed when the activity is introduced, it generally brings about some good laughs and high-fives when things don't end with someone falling on their butt.

From my perspective, there are three types of players in this game. The first type is the "what the hell, let's do this thing" player. This individual stands up straight, keeps their head up, knees locked, arms firmly raised, and gracefully falls back as if there is absolutely no doubt in their mind they will be caught.

The second type is the "I don't want to do this, but they'll judge me if I don't" player. This individual is nervously giggling and perspiring; they attempt to fall backward *safely.* It's pretty comical to watch. They will continue to turn around to ensure the person behind them is perfectly lined up and ready to catch them. Their knees are slightly bent, and their arms are positioned slightly behind them (in case they need to catch themselves on the fly). The best part is when they start to fall back, their arms flail, which gives them the sense of being out of control, so they actually fall to the ground before their partner has a chance to catch them.

And the third type is the "hell no, this is ridiculous" player. This individual will refuse to play and stand on the sidelines, arms folded against their chest, observing everyone else.

How you do one thing is how you do everything.

Which player are you in the game of life? And, more importantly, which player do you want to be?

Could it be possible that a failure to commit comes not only from a lack of trust in our resolve to do what we say we're going to do but also from an overwhelming belief that it won't work out? Anytime you think about a future event, you imagine a moment that doesn't exist yet. Do you spend most of your time imagining the worst, or do you use your power of imagination to picture great success?

We often don't allow ourselves to fully commit to seeing an inner dream or desire through because we're so busy trying to control the outcome, preparing for the worst, and avoiding pain (especially the sting of failure).

This can lead to a vicious cycle of "will I or won't I," which consumes tremendous energy. Have you ever battled to make an important life decision, going back and forth, listing the pros and cons, and asking advice from all your friends? It's exhausting. Generally, when you finally come to a decision, or the Universe forces your hand, the outcome is such a relief because you are no longer spending all your energy trying to make a decision.

You must decide to *go all in* on your deepest dreams and desires—no back doors, no plan B, and no sitting on the sidelines. You've got to stand up, say, "Oh, what the hell," and let yourself fall. The moment the Universe catches you is worth every second of fear you had before making the commitment.

Here are a few tips on how to strengthen that commitment and increase your chances of getting the results you want.

HOW YOU BEGIN IS HOW YOU END

Let's talk about the importance of *beginnings*; this is not something they teach you in school, so pay attention. The energy and intent you bring to a project, relationship, or experience become the foundation and, ultimately, the result. As discussed in Chapter 4: Manifest Your New Vision, we are energetic beings living in an energetic Universe; thus, our vibrational energy is channeled into whatever we are creating.

Why is this important? Because your energetic state is infused into what you are creating and can positively or negatively affect its impact on others.

Email is my favorite example of this. Have you ever opened up an email from a client or superior and automatically felt negative emotions? The words were probably written in a neutral tone, but something about that email made you feel heightened emotion within seconds. Alternatively, have you ever received an email that feels like a warm, energetic hug?

We communicate through our energy far more than our words. Think about the last big project or initiative you worked on. How were you feeling at the time? Were you having fun, feeling optimistic and excited about its impact, or were you stressing, anxious, and doubtful of its success? Any form of negativity and fear you are feeling becomes the weeds that grow next to the flower, stealing the natural resources that would allow a full, beautiful bloom.

Once you put your stake in the sand and commit to doing something, your next step is to clear the soil and pull those damn weeds—*before* you plant the seed of your idea.

I often host trainings for the company I work for, addressing the limiting beliefs and fears that could skew the attendees' intended results and teaching them how to release these blocks to their success. While it's ideal to do this before initiating a project or relationship, it's never too late to correct it.

SET YOUR INTENTION

The next step is to make sure your intention is as pure and high-vibe as possible. Before you begin anything, you should declare an intention that will guide your results. Do not, under any circumstances, skip this step.

Commitment and intention go hand in hand; one without the other is just a pipe dream. Your intention encapsulates your why and the results you want to achieve.

Would you go to a restaurant, sit down at a table, and place your order without looking at the menu? Or would you give your server a really vague request like "Maybe bring me some meat and vegetables"? No, you would look at the options, decide what feels the most appealing to you, and then place a specific order for exactly what you want.

You need to bring that same approach to pretty much everything. Before I start a meeting, I take a minute to refine my intention for what I want the outcome to be. Before I go to bed, I set my intention for how I want to feel when I wake up. Before I started this book, and every time I sat down to write, I set an intention that the words will flow and will have the greatest impact on those who connect with this book.

Author, coach, and internationally renowned motivational speaker Tony Robbins teaches, "Stay committed to your decisions but flexible in your approach." This means that you must hold firm to your intention but not fixate on the how. Your intention becomes the instructions for what you want to achieve and how you want to feel when you do. All the details of *how* that happens are co-created with an all-knowing, all-loving Universe and will probably materialize in a way that you least expect.

MOMENTUM

In my experience, once you commit to something, you go through rites of initiation. It's almost as if the Universe wants to test your resolve and *make sure* you're going for it no matter what. These little tests can appear as closed doors, rejections, a lack of sales, and lots of naysayers.

Rudi and I love to watch *The Voice* with our kids. We enjoy watching aspiring singers show up and sing their hearts out every week, although it can be heartbreaking to see the tears when they are voted off the show as it gets closer to the finale. There can only be one winner each season, so what will happen to all the contestants who clawed and fought their way onto that stage?

Will that be the end of their aspirations to be a famous artist who tours the world, or will that experience create enough momentum to move them to the next step toward their intended outcome?

Momentum is a term in physics that translates to "mass in motion." It relates to the relationship between speed, mass, and direction. Essentially, if you increase the mass or velocity (i.e., speed) of an object, the momentum of the object increases in the direction it is traveling. Although incredibly small, a bullet has a tremendous amount of momentum because of its extreme speed.

In life, you are the mass, and your actions are the velocity. Your size is fixed; however, what impacts your momentum is taking continued daily action. A journey that at first feels slow and labored will start to quicken as you build one action on top of another. Eventually, you will create so much speed that even taking the littlest action can quantum leap you forward.

I love the experience of shifting comfortably into the *momentum flow*. All of a sudden, what seemed to be a boulder I was pushing uphill starts to roll effortlessly down the other side, and I get to run alongside with minimal effort. The thing is, to experience the downhill, you've got to first commit to the uphill and not give up a few feet from the peak.

Stay the course of your desire. Commit to taking daily action, no matter what.

DON'T OVERCOMMIT

I have to share an important disclaimer: don't try to move forward with too many desires at one time.

You have a finite amount of energy, and your focus is one of the most powerful tools you have at your disposal to manifest your desires. If you have a list of ten priority goals that you want to work on all at once, you're diluting the force of your energy and, thus, the results.

I'm so guilty of this. I'm a multitasker by nature, so it's incredibly tempting to look at my vision board and want it *all* right now. I've learned that when I'm stacking my plate too high with everything, it's a symptom of avoiding what I should be doing out of fear.

I see this a lot with individuals who want to start a business or a side hustle. They spend all their time building their program, product, and website, but fail to do the one thing that will create clients: *speaking to people.*

They will avoid sales calls like the plague, but if they would just dedicate a few hours a day to getting on the phone and having conversations, the momentum would build, and one day, they would wake up and realize they have a profitable business.

Pick one to two goals or major tasks to work on at a time. Many people overestimate what they can do in a year, get overwhelmed, and don't achieve anything on their list. That said, many people underestimate what they can do in three years. Let's do the math: If you chose four goals to work toward each year for three years, that's *twelve* significant achievements in three years! That's enough to transform your life completely. And even better, with every ninety-day completion, how confident and unlimited would you feel? Your goals would just get bigger and more expansive, right?

Here's what I know to be true: If you give yourself twelve months, you'll take twelve months, but if you give yourself ninety days, you'll complete it in ninety days. But that only works if you tackle *one* big, scary goal at a time.

Life is a *journey*, and you should continue to expand and grow. You will have a never-ending stream of desires that come through you and catalyze your next level of learning and growth, but it requires developing the level of commitment necessary to initiate and bring them to completion.

If you've had a hard time keeping your commitments in the past, that's okay. Be kind to yourself. You get to change that belief about yourself. You get to be the person who keeps your commitments—especially to yourself—and you can start *today.*

Once you are fully committed to fulfilling your purpose, no number of setbacks, obstacles, time issues, or rejections will stop you. When you no longer question *if* you will, you just keep showing up, knowing that eventually, at the perfect time, you will achieve what you set out to do.

This begins the cycle of creating your calling—one inspiration leading to another until, eventually, you turn back and are in awe at how far you've come and the ripple effect you have created in the world.

PUTTING IT INTO PRACTICE

If you become adept at keeping small commitments to yourself daily, you will have a greater chance of keeping the big ones when it matters. What follows are some steps and strategies to help you stay committed.

1. Keep a commitment journal. I prefer a small notepad I can carry in my pocket or handbag.
2. Every morning, write out one to three small tasks or actions you are committing to take and give yourself a deadline. For example: "Today, I commit to thirty minutes of exercise on my Peloton, scheduling a sales call with X client, and spending twenty minutes playing Candy Land with my kids after work."
3. Mark off your committed action as soon as it's achieved. Take a moment to feel the joy of keeping your commitment to yourself (I like to pump my fist and say, "*Yes!*").
4. If you haven't kept your commitments, ask yourself why. What got in the way? What fear or limiting belief might be lurking there? Just as there's a benefit to completing your commitments, you can improve your self-awareness when you don't.

Chapter 12

SURRENDER AND LET GO

Surrender and accept that whatever is happening in the moment, the Universe is working on your behalf.

—Mastin Kipp, Author, Speaker, and Creator of Functional Life Coaching

WHEN I REFLECT ON MY journey, I am in constant awe of everything that has brought me to where I am today. It's so easy to look back and see how all my experiences have been connected and perfectly timed. Yet, when I zoom in on the minute details of everyday life, it is easy to question if my dreams and desires are valid and if I will ever reach them.

I believe that you tap into a supernatural magic when you answer the calling of your soul. This magic activates a Universal assistance that is indescribable and often indiscernible to the naked eye. Once you have committed to act on your purpose, you are setting something into motion. You will align with the resources, experiences, opportunities, and mentors needed to move to the next step as long as you don't waver from that commitment.

All that is required from you is a willingness to surrender your need to *see* and *know* what's going on behind the scenes, to let go of how you think your journey should look, and to trust that whatever emerges is the perfect match for your intention. You can't do this alone, nor should you want to, as you have a narrow scope of possibilities and potential available to you.

We are all connected in this vast Universe; there is an all-knowing source coordinating the timing of your desire to meet someone else's need, and vice versa. When you say, "I need money," it could simultaneously compel someone else to repay a debt they owe you. When you feel inspired to write a book, someone else could be asking for the very information flowing through you onto the page. When you need health advice, someone else is giving a lecture on that very topic and sends you an email invite.

Don't you see? This all-knowing Universe we live in is magical and ready to support us in fulfilling our destiny. Muster up the courage to accept that you don't know everything; hand over the reins, and prepare for the most amazing ride of your life! There will be unexpected twists and turns, exhilarating ups and downs, and daily miracles.

Our minds are generally not the best navigators when it comes to charting the direction of our purpose; this is because our brains are geared toward protection and forecasting based on past experiences. Our minds will judge what is happening as right or wrong, good or bad, instead of accepting *what is* as perfect and right on time. You are venturing into the great unknown, so you must trust that where you are guided will be precisely where you need to be.

In bestselling author Michael A. Singer's book *The Surrender Experiment,* he shares his story of undergoing a profound spiritual awakening and deciding not to let his personal opinions, fears, and desires dictate the direction of his life. Instead, he surrendered to whatever life had in store. Singer writes, "I clearly remember deciding that from now on, if life was unfolding in a certain way, and the only reason I was resisting it was because of a personal preference, I would let go of my preference and let life be in charge." He thought his destiny was just a minuscule part of what his soul had intended; getting out of the way created an extraordinary impact, abundance, and the deep satisfaction and fulfillment he was seeking.

Singer's faith was tested with every unexpected experience and opportunity. He was constantly pushed out of his comfort zone, battling fears of uncertainty, imposter syndrome, and failure. Yet, he had committed to fulfilling the highest expression of his purpose, and he knew it would require him to suspend all judgment and say a big, fat *yes* to life.

Many years ago, Rudi and I participated in our own surrender experiment. We had just moved to Wilmington, North Carolina, fulfilling an intention we had set five years prior. Rudi had left the day-to-day workings of his company in Cincinnati to his partner and was preparing to move full-time into writing, speaking, and coaching. He was clear on his purpose and what he felt he was here to do, but was willing to leave the how, when, where, and who up to the Universe.

A few weeks after starting our own surrender experiment, Rudi received an unexpected job opportunity with the same Miami-based company I was working for remotely at the time. The position involved overseeing and leading their entire sales team, but Rudi wasn't looking for a job. That was the *last* thing he wanted. He had worked hard to move out of Corporate America, and no part of him wanted to return. So, he politely declined.

They called again to sweeten the deal, and again, Rudi said no. They were so sure that Rudi was the perfect guy for the job that they were willing to make a third offer and risk another rejection. At that point, Rudi couldn't ignore that this opportunity had come out of nowhere and fallen in his lap, tied with a beautiful bow. It not-so-coincidentally came after setting the intention to surrender to what life put on his path. Yet, his mind kept telling him this was a massive detour from the direction he *should* be heading and would amount to a step backward. It would require us to move to Miami, just months after finally moving to a city we love, and neither of us was excited at the prospect.

The signs that something unexpected was coming had appeared months before—we didn't know what they meant at the time. We had intended to buy a house in Wilmington and had made three separate offers on homes that all fell through. We'd immediately fallen in love with the first house we saw and asked our realtor to prepare an offer. As we were driving away from that showing, a freak tornado came through the area and twirled straight through the back of the house. Our realtor called to let us know the owners had taken it off the market to make repairs, and it would be at least six to eight months before it went back on the market.

Disappointed but determined, we made an offer on another home the next day. That home had been on the market for almost a year with zero offers in months. As she prepared and submitted our offer, our realtor predicted it would be a slam dunk. A few minutes later, she received a call from the seller's realtor, informing her the owners had received and accepted an offer an hour before we submitted ours. We weren't particularly excited about the third home, but we submitted an offer anyway, and they accepted. Lo and behold, when the house inspection was complete, the report indicated almost six figures in repairs would be required. The owner was unwilling to pay a dime, so we canceled the contract. We had already sold our existing home in Cincinnati and had two weeks to move out. So, with no other options, we decided to find a property we could lease for a year.

Rejection is always *redirection*. We were blocked from buying a home—that was clear. I mean, a tornado coming out of nowhere on a sunny day? You can't make this shit up! An event like that has fate's fingerprints all over it. So, when Rudi's job offer came out of nowhere and would require us to move, we had the sneaky suspicion this had been the Universe's plan all along. If we had bought a home, it would not have been as easy to pick up and go.

Ultimately, Rudi said yes to the job, and we moved to Miami for two years before returning to Wilmington. It required a *massive* leap of faith for both of us, but looking back, it was exactly what we needed. The opportunity he had been asking for—the one that would catapult him into *being* a successful coach and impacting the world—came disguised as a job. For the next two years, he got to show up as a powerful, transformational coach and bring personal development and mindset into a corporate setting. When it was time to move on, he was amply prepared and qualified to launch an impactful coaching business that now serves hundreds of individuals and companies. He is coaching high-level executives into self-leadership and the ability to elevate their team's performance, job satisfaction, and company culture.

Our life is exactly how we envisioned it, full of abundance, freedom, fulfillment, and joy. But we never could have imagined the path it would take to get here. Now, when we have a desire, we are happy to hand it over to the Universe and trust it will come as it should.

As poet and spiritual advisor Mark Nepo once said, "Surrender is like a fish finding the current and going with it." Fulfilling your purpose doesn't have to be a struggle. It can be *easy* once you've mastered the art of surrender, letting go, and trusting.

SURRENDER

So much of our pain, resistance, and negative emotion comes from holding too tightly to an outcome. We judge and hold an opinion on everything: "It should be this way or that," or "They are wrong," or "That shouldn't have happened." The thing is—it did happen. The fact that something occurred means it was meant to happen. I don't believe the Universe creates accidents. I know this can be hard to fathom, considering the horrible things we see, like starving children, sex trafficking, and school shootings. No sane person would ever like, condone, or support such terrible acts. So, how do we surrender our judgment?

SURRENDER IS ACCEPTANCE

When you resist an experience, person, or thing, you are essentially pushing against it, thinking it shouldn't be there, missing the point that *it is there.* So, if it is there, ask *why.* Acceptance doesn't mean staying in an experience or situation that is harmful to you. It means trusting that there is a lesson in the experience and actively looking for it.

We learn through experiences that force us to grow and expand; experiences we don't want or expect are opportunities to learn. What I have come to believe is every experience is happening *for* us, even when it comes disguised as something ugly and terrible. When you can believe that there are no wasted moments and everything has a place and purpose, you can benefit from the relief gained from accepting what is. To accept life as it happens is a gateway to effortlessly flowing with your purpose and experiencing true peace. What you resist persists. You can learn from what you accept and then make the appropriate choices to move forward.

Adopting an attitude of acceptance doesn't mean that *every* experience that pops up in your awareness should get a resounding yes from you. For instance, in Rudi's case, the opportunity continued to come, and when he checked in with himself to see if it felt aligned, it did. His mind told him that this looked different from how he envisioned launching his coaching career. But his heart was telling him, "This is the way."

As discussed at the beginning of this book, when you know the difference between what is in and out of alignment with your purpose, you can more easily surrender to what is coming. While it might not look right, it will *feel* right.

I hope that you will very soon get to a point where you are weary of the pain, stress, and anxiety caused by trying to control the uncontrollable and that you will throw up your hands and say, "You do it!" That will be the sacred moment when you are ready to let go and hand over the reins to an all-knowing, all-powerful force. Let me assure you—you are in good hands!

When you can accept where you are and who you are in this very moment, you are pulling up the resistance anchor that has been holding you in place. Then, you can follow your heart's desire, surrender to the current, and trust that the speed and direction are perfect to transport you to the next stop on your journey.

But first, you'll have to *let go* of those oars.

LET GO

Many years ago, while meditating, I received an answer to a question I had been asking the Universe. I was in a funk and felt like I was hitting challenges at every turn. My question was, "Why does this have to be so hard?"

The vision I received was of two hands, both squeezed tight into fists. And an inner voice said, "You have to let go to let the light flow in." I opened my eyes, looked at my hands, and received the knowledge that I had been holding so tight to what was and this vision I had for my future that it was blocking the Universal flow of inspiration, resources, abundance, and love. I just needed to loosen my grip enough to let my intentions be made manifest.

I challenge you to try this exercise right now in order to imprint this lesson on your mind and memory. I want you to think of an area of your life where you are worried, struggling, facing challenges, confused, unsure of what to do next. As you hold this scene in your mind, clench both fists, feeling the intensity of your desire for a positive result. Notice how the strength of your hands can come together so tightly that if you held them under running water, the water would not reach the inside of your fist but would instead run off the sides. Begin to release your clenched fists, and imagine liquid light running through your hands and around your fingertips. Now, life is in motion again and working for your good.

Do you see how fear causes constriction? It is human nature to hold tightly to what is when we fear the unknown. Clinging to a specific outcome like our life depends on it creates an energetic dam, preventing a river of blessings and answered prayers from flowing your way.

This vision I received was gold, and I practiced this exercise whenever I found myself worrying and stressing about something. The result was a feeling of deep peace and faith in the Universe to protect and provide. I felt instantaneous relief and joy with each reminder that I am not alone and that we live in a friendly Universe, here to support, not punish.

You can learn all the things, take all the right actions, and set yourself up for success in every way possible. But if you fail to learn the art of letting go, it will all be for nothing. Plus, you will sign yourself up for a long trip on the struggle bus!

Letting go isn't just necessary for your career, relationships, health, and finances. It is also about letting go of aspects of *yourself*. Becoming who you want to be will require you to overcome the limiting beliefs and behaviors that have kept you anchored in the past.

To move your life toward your calling, you will be required to change physically and energetically. You have to become what you seek, and that might require letting go of some of the personal qualities with which you identify.

For example, when I started taking accelerated action toward becoming a spiritual teacher, I knew I would have to let go of my tendency to hide and avoid being seen, as well as my belief that I wasn't entrepreneur material. These were beliefs about myself that had become a part of my identity. They were not fixed qualities, just thoughts I had agreed with at some point, and thus, they became a part of who I thought I was.

Rudi and I take our clients through an exercise of examining the current beliefs they hold about themselves and investigating whether they are accurate and align with their purpose. If they are not, we ask the client to create a new agreement based on who they *choose* to be.

You get to let go of negative beliefs about yourself. You get to rewrite, refine, and redefine who you are and how you show up in this world.

I have a quote on my office wall from the *Tao of Leadership* by John Heider, an adaptation of ancient Chinese philosopher Lao Tzu's teachings for modern business leaders: "When I let go of what I am, I become what I might be." Just as we hold tightly to our life circumstances, wishes, and specific outcomes, we also clench our fists around the identities we have unknowingly created for ourselves.

What would happen if you were to let go of who you believe yourself to be? While fulfilling your purpose is the key to personal fulfillment, this is the path to true *transformation*. You get to see yourself anew as the light illuminates your true nature: an unlimited, free, abundant, co-creative spirit having a human experience. You get to see that all your perceived limitations and weaknesses were just illusions. When you cross over the threshold and look back, you will, as John Heider suggests in *The Tao of Leadership*, "become what you might be."

You have a vision for what you want. Hold on to the essence of that vision, whether it be abundance, freedom, love, or happiness. Let go of the how and allow the all-powerful, all-knowing Universe to flow to you and through you, bringing the perfect match to your desire.

Let go and *trust,* over and over again.

TRUST

After Rudi and I married, we decided to wait two years before having a baby. I lasted about eighteen months before getting broody and anxious about getting the baby-making train started. I began changing my eating habits and workout routine to align with what I would do once I was pregnant. About three months before the two-year mark, I stopped taking birth control, and then the excitement and heightened watch on my cycle began. My first thought in the morning and the last before dozing off to sleep was, "Am I pregnant yet?" The desire to be a mother overtook my world like a tsunami, and it was hard to focus on anything else.

I read all the blogs and books on increasing my odds of getting pregnant and checked to see if I was ovulating almost daily. When I got my period, I cried. I was so disappointed and let down. It had only been a month, but it was enough of a blow to make me doubt that this would work. Maybe I couldn't or wouldn't ever get pregnant. Before that moment, I had no reason to doubt my ability to conceive. It was so out of my control that it drove me crazy. Rudi, of course, was like, "Chill out! It's only been thirty days," which made it even worse because I felt like I was shouldering the weight of our dream alone.

Two days before our second anniversary, on Rudi's birthday, I found out I was pregnant. Instantly, I went from worrying, anxious, and doubting about conceiving to knowing a child was on the way. The shift in my energy and inner narrative was remarkable. I immediately dropped the old thoughts and replaced them with "Where should we find a crib?" and "I wonder if it's a boy or a girl!"

Ultimately, we are all pregnant with our desires. They were born from within us. We don't need to pine for them or worry about their development or when they will be ready to be delivered. Unfortunately, and fortunately, that is all out of our control.

Why not skip the part of allowing yourself to go crazy with doubt and fear that it will never come—at least not in the form you think it should—and jump right to the part where you know it is happening and you get to prepare for the birth? When you can trust that what is happening behind the scenes is being handled by an expert director, you can release the need for control. You can sit in the theater with excited expectations, eating your popcorn and waiting for the coming attractions.

Your journey to the highest vision of your life will look different from how you expect it to. A few moments here and there might come to pass as you imagined, but ultimately, it will be one surprising, synchronistic, "holy shit" moment after another. Remember, life isn't about the destination but about who you become on the journey. This journey to your purpose will stretch your faith, expand your boundaries, and create a beautiful relationship with the invisible, divine intelligence of the Universe.

Your life can become a dance of bringing forward your desire, acting when inspired, committing to holding the vision, and then surrendering to your all-knowing partner who will bring it to you in the perfect package.

PUTTING IT INTO PRACTICE

1. Take out your journal and list all the most remarkable experiences, relationships, gifts, and opportunities you have received.
2. Go back to the top of your list and write down how each came to you. Was it the result of an intention or desire? Or did it just come out of nowhere and fall into your lap? Did it look like you imagined it would or was it different? Was it better or worse?
3. Finally, what did you gain from each situation? How did each contribute to who you are today?

Part 4

STAY ON TRACK

Chapter 13

FEEL YOUR WAY FORWARD

Have the courage to follow your heart and intuition. They somehow already know what you truly want to become.

—Steve Jobs, American Businessman, Inventor, CEO of Apple Inc.

NOW THAT YOU'RE COMMITTED TO living a life aligned with your purpose, you must arm yourself with tools to support you in embodying this new way of being. Self-sabotaging habits and limiting beliefs will occasionally show up, but please know this is normal. You've spent a long time being *you,* which means it'll take some time to create and embody new ways of being. I call this the in-between state, and it can feel seriously foreign and uncomfortable. I want to provide a few ideas, tools, and tactics that have supported me and many others on this journey.

One powerful tool you already have access to is your internal guidance system. In addition to keeping you out of harm's way, its job is to lead you toward that which is aligned with your purpose and destiny. I love this quote from spiritual author Neale Donald Walsch: "Built into you is an internal guidance system that shows you the way home. All you need to do is heed the voice."

Your internal guidance system isn't located in your brain but in your *heart.*

YOUR HEART IS YOUR GUIDE

Your heart has been whispering to you since birth—reminding you of your purpose for this lifetime and how capable you are of achieving it.

Your heart is the keeper of your dreams, desires, and destiny and will always guide you toward what is best for you.

Your heart will encourage you to go for it. At the same time, your mind will try to keep you within what it deems safe (i.e., inside your comfort zone and far away from the potential to fail, be judged, or feel any negative emotion).

Think back to a time in your life when you heeded your heart's guidance; how did that turn out for you? I would bet that even if you didn't get the outcome you were hoping for, you felt a sense of accomplishment and peace that at least you had tried. What about a time in your life when you followed your head and ignored the pleadings of your heart? I would bet that, in the end, you felt regret and disappointment. Your mind pulls from the past to predict what is possible, while your heart knows there are infinite ways to reach your highest potential.

To fully align with your purpose, you will have to make a *big* decision. Are you willing to start trusting your heart as your guide? If you decide to follow your mind, know that it will try to keep you safe at the cost of accomplishing your dreams. It will want you to stay within your comfort zone, doing the same thing you've always done. And it will tell you the yearnings of your heart are crazy and irresponsible.

For those brave souls ready to lead a heart-led life, buckle up—you're about to forge your path forward. Your life will undoubtedly be full of adventure, joy, love, and *life.* Your heart doesn't follow a rule book, and it loves to color outside the lines—it's like that crazy friend that your parents were petrified of you hanging out with in high school. But know it loves you unconditionally and only wants the best for you. The reward of following your heart is peace, joy, fulfillment, and a life of purpose.

In this game called life, you can't follow two masters. You have to choose between your mind and your heart—unless, of course, they are *aligned.*

ALIGN YOUR HEART AND MIND

I grew up believing that my brain was the great conductor—constantly sending signals and directions to all parts of my body. However, science has shown that the heart sends more signals to the brain than the brain does to the heart.

In 1991, Dr. Andrew Armour published an abstract in the *Cleveland Clinic Journal of Medicine* titled "The Little Brain on the Heart." He discovered that the heart has a "little brain" with over 40,000 neurons, similar to those in the brain. This means the heart has its *own* nervous system, sensing and responding to external stimuli. The vagus nerve then carries information from the heart and other organs into the brain. In fact, your heart often responds to external stimuli *before* your brain does.

According to the HeartMath Institute, the heart's signals to the brain greatly influence how we process emotion and other cognitive functions like focus, memory, and problem-solving. Your heart rate becomes erratic when you're under stress and feeling negative emotions. Thus, the signals going to your brain become disordered and unclear, inhibiting your cognitive abilities and reinforcing and prolonging emotional instability.

On the flip side, when experiencing heightened positive emotions, your heart sends beautiful, clear signals to the brain that enhance and elevate your cognitive abilities and strengthen positive feelings, allowing you to experience *more* of them.

In the 1990s, HeartMath researchers identified a physiological state called heart coherence. This state occurs when our body's systems, such as heart rhythm, breathing, blood pressure, and hormonal response, are in sync, positively affecting our physical, mental, and emotional states. When your heart rate gets orderly and coherent, it energizes the brain and acts as an amplifier.

Think of a day in your life when everything just seemed to flow. You felt *great.* Your mind was clear, and you were in an elevated, optimistic mood. You felt excited about your life and confident about your future. You could handle challenges gracefully and didn't let outside triggers knock you from your positive mood. On this day, your heart and brain were in coherence.

Your brain and your heart will be at odds with each other if they are not working in coherence. Your brain will not function well if you're feeling stressed, triggered, anxious, and overwhelmed. Think of it this way: If your heart is closed down due to negative emotions and stress, so is your brain.

Living a purpose-driven life requires you to lean on your heart to guide you forward; your brain needs to be open to receive creative ideas and inspiration. When your heart and brain are aligned, you're poised to express your true zone of genius.

Heart coherence is the key to *being* the highest, best version of yourself, and here's the great news: You can sync up your heart and brain yourself! Heart coherence can be self-regulated.

What if it was as easy as spending ten to fifteen minutes in the morning generating positive emotions in your heart—feeling love, freedom, gratitude, abundance, and joy? What if you took up that gratitude practice you've been putting off and committed to writing twenty things that you're grateful for every morning while sipping your coffee? What if you could become aware of negative emotions or stress in the middle of your day and decide to take ten minutes to put on upbeat music and take a walk so you could feel better?

You are in the driver's seat of how you feel—*always*. No one and nothing can *make* you feel a certain way. You get to choose how you respond to any experience. When you practice relaxing your heart back into a neutral, calm state after feeling triggered, you train your brain and body to self-regulate.

When your heart is relaxed and your brain is open, it becomes easier to hear and follow your internal guidance system, leading you toward your desired future.

TRUST YOUR HEART

To trust your heart, you have to start speaking its language. While your brain communicates through thought, your heart communicates through *feeling*.

You're constantly receiving feedback from your heart on how you feel—the question is, are you paying attention? Sometimes, we let our thoughts drown out our feelings, trusting our minds over our hearts. Other times, we acknowledge a feeling but ignore it because we don't understand its message.

I learned how to translate my heart's language in my early twenties. I remember for months fighting the feeling in my heart that told me I needed to break up with my college boyfriend. Eventually, it got so strong that I couldn't ignore it anymore. I didn't understand it, as we were great together and he was fantastic. But my heart knew he wasn't my forever, and I eventually had to surrender to that feeling without my brain knowing why. Your heart is all-knowing and will tell you when to let go of relationships and experiences that aren't right for you. It's when we fight or ignore those feelings that *suffering* begins in the form of depression, anxiety, frustration, resentment, and a sense of being lost.

Your heart will guide you when to let go and when to begin and take impactful actions to move you forward.

While it was easy to trust my heart, it was hard to learn the courage to *act* on my heart's instructions. For many years, I've practiced automatic writing in the morning. I will write a question on the top of a blank page in my journal and then write whatever comes to my mind without judgment or editing.

I ask, "What do I most need to know or do today for my highest good?"

Sometimes, the information that comes is related to an issue I was dealing with the day before or in the form of a powerful reminder of my divinity and limitless nature. But some days, what comes out is an idea, a project, or a video I should record and post online. Even as the idea flows onto the page, I can feel my mind start to butt in and tell me all the reasons I should *not* do this—all fear-based, limiting beliefs. Some days, I fall prey to the mind's fears and bail entirely on the inspired ideas, leaving them to rot on the page.

However, on the days I have the courage to follow through with the inspired action, I feel so freaking powerful and accomplished. And often, I'll receive validation that it was the right decision. For example, I once followed my heart's urging to post a specific message online. I grabbed my phone and did it right away. A few hours later, I received a message from someone saying it was *exactly* what they had needed to hear. My inspiration that day was the answer to someone else's silent request for help. We are all beautifully connected, and that connection speaks through our hearts.

As discussed in Chapter 10: Take Inspir-action, learning to take inspired, heart-led action *is* the way to fulfill your purpose.

You're building a relationship with your heart, and just like in any relationship, what you put in is what you get back. You need to create the space to listen to your heart. What does its voice sound like? Feel like? How is it different from the voice that is coming from your mind?

Your heart's guidance will often be at odds with what your mind is telling you and it might not make logical sense. Think about it this way: Your heart is connected to your soul and it has a higher vantage point than you do. While you might not see the relevance or importance of taking a specific action, your heart is connected to all the Universe's potentials. It is nudging you down this path for a reason, because it knows it to be best. You're going to have to act in faith before you understand what that reason is.

STAY ALIGNED

A great sign that you are on the right path is positive emotion and feeling.

I've had seasons wherein I didn't *love* what I was doing in my job, but when I checked in with my heart, I felt a sense of peace and satisfaction. That's my heart's language for, "You're exactly where you need to be right now." I've also had an experience where I was working for a company and found myself feeling frustrated, dissatisfied, and bored. It would be best to treat these feelings like the blinking check engine light on your dashboard—no need to panic, but *don't ignore it*, lest you wind up broken down on the side of the road in the middle of the night. In that particular situation, I did ignore it; I tried to repress these feelings for too long, fighting them with thoughts that it would be silly to leave a solid, high-paying job.

Eventually, that icky feeling I had at work started to spill over into other areas of my life; my health suffered, I didn't sleep well, and I was cranky with Rudi and the kids. It wasn't a good look—and I was tired of getting sick and feeling that way.

So, what did I do? As much as I wanted to march into my boss's office to offer my resignation, enjoying the instant gratification of being free of that situation, I didn't.

Thankfully, I knew better. I decided to start by focusing on the only place that could create the change I was seeking—inside. First, I had to take full accountability for how I was feeling. I had chosen to take that job and stay as long as I had. No one had handcuffed me to my desk, even though I felt the invisible, self-imposed handcuffs around my wrists.

Next, I intentionally changed my inner dialogue. I used powerful questions to obtain the answers to why I was feeling this way. Rather than asking myself, "How can I get out of this job to start feeling better?" I asked, "Why am I feeling this way right now?" and, "What are my feelings trying to tell me?"

I discovered that somewhere along the way, I had stopped looking for the purpose in my present situation and started resisting it. The job I once loved hadn't changed—I had changed how I perceived it. I was fighting with what is, spending my time focusing on where I wanted to be, simultaneously feeling the pain of not having achieved it yet.

During this time of self-inquiry, I also discovered—and finally admitted to myself—that I was ready for something different. I realized I had perceived that energetic shift as "This job now sucks" instead of "It might be time to prepare to move to the next step on my journey." Rather than remaining grateful for my current job and holding positive expectations for a new opportunity to come my way, I pushed against it and made it the enemy. This was a big aha moment.

This small change in perception created a massive shift in how I felt and approached my current job. I relaxed and began to enjoy my job again—I knew it wasn't my forever, just my reality for right now. I trusted that I was exactly where I needed to be and that there was still something to learn from this job experience. But when it was time to go, I would walk forward in faith. A few weeks later, my boss approached me and asked me to assist with a big project. It was challenging and exciting, and I was grateful to leave work every day with a feeling of accomplishment and fulfillment. I was so busy that I barely noticed the months flying by, and I had all but forgotten about wanting to leave my job.

A few months later, I received two job offers in one week. Both of these offers came out of nowhere and were terrific opportunities. I accepted the one that felt most aligned with my purpose and, with nothing but love and gratitude in my heart, offered my resignation.

This story is just one of millions of examples of how you can fall out of alignment with your path—and what it looks like to self-correct. It *will* happen. But once you learn to trust your heart, the time it takes to self-correct will become increasingly shorter. Once you get used to experiencing the positive state of being aligned with your purpose, you will have little patience for the yucky feelings of misalignment.

What follows are common symptoms of being out of alignment with your heart:

- Feeling off, lost, and stuck
- Lack of excitement about what you're doing and where you're going
- Experiencing resistance in the form of obstacles, challenges, and ongoing delays
- Frustration and resentment
- Being overly concerned about what others think

Staying aligned requires a great deal of self-awareness. You have to deeply know *yourself, be able to* easily identify when you start feeling these symptoms, and be willing to take the action needed to start feeling better.

A great way to do this is to focus on what brings you joy.

FIND RELIEF WITH JOY

I love this quote from American spiritual influencer and author Teal Swan: "Sample things and follow the sensation of relief, and you will find your joy. Find joy and follow it, and you will find your purpose."

As discussed in Chapter 2: Revise Your Resume, doing what brings you joy will point you in the direction of your authentic self. And if you're having a hard time understanding any negative feelings, busy yourself doing something that brings you joy. This will bring you quick relief and dissolve any resistance to receiving clarity and inspiration for your next steps.

I totally get that shifting your focus from the problem to creating, doing, or experiencing something that brings you joy can feel *wrong*. I mean, if you're not working overtime to fix the problem, who will? Trust me, the longer you can take your focus off of it, the better.

I can't tell you how often I've intentionally pried my attention away from something causing me pain and turned it to a creative project, only to return to the problem and find it had either completely dissolved or resolved itself. Doing what brings you love elevates your energy, and maybe, just maybe, you'll find you're now an energetic match for the solution.

Joy is a powerful sign of alignment. Follow your joy and honor its guidance.

PUTTING IT INTO PRACTICE

Set aside some time to listen to your heart's guidance. When you make space for this voice, it will get louder and become a full-on dialogue throughout the day.

1. Grab a journal and pen (and a cup of coffee or tea if you choose).
2. Open to a blank page and, at the top, write one of the following questions:

- What do I need to know today for my highest and greatest good?
- What are my feelings about X trying to tell me?
- What am I not seeing clearly right now?
- What do I need to do to align with my purpose today?

3. Write down whatever words come to you without stopping and without judgment. Write until your mind grows quiet again and then read what you wrote aloud.
4. Contemplate your answer. Think about it throughout your day and see if more information comes.

The answer to all of your questions can be found within you. If you create the time and space to receive, you will see just how wise and all-knowing your heart is.

This simple practice is a powerful way for you to *feel your way forward,* staying aligned with your destiny today, tomorrow, and for the rest of your life.

Chapter 14

JOIN THE UNIVERSE'S PAYROLL

Like the air you breathe, abundance in all things is available to you. Your life will simply be as good as you allow it to be.

—Ester Hicks, American Inspirational Speaker, Author, and Cofounder of Abraham-Hicks Publications

WHEN RUDI AND I FIRST met, one of the many traits I was so impressed by was his relationship with money. He had this daily practice wherein he would pick up spare change on the ground, close his eyes, and say, "Money comes to me quickly and easily." At first, my response was, "Ew, you just touched a dirty coin on the ground, and it's only a penny; what are you going to do with that?!"

He explained that money comes to him in all ways. When he fails to accept and honor even the smallest gift (e.g., dirty pennies on the ground), he blocks the flow of abundance from coming in other ways. This was a new idea for me. Until then, if I passed some change on the street, I wouldn't bother picking it up, thinking there's bound to be someone else who needs it more than me. But the point I was missing is that, out of the hundreds and thousands of people who walked past those coins, I noticed them—so maybe they were meant for me.

Rudi has always been incredibly abundant, attracting and making money with ease. But that wasn't my experience up until that point. Don't get me wrong, I had managed to make enough money to support myself and live a comfortable life, but making money had always felt hard, inconsistent, and stressful.

Soon after getting married, we bought a home and immediately started furnishing and renovating the basement. We spent *a lot* of money in a short amount of time, and it was freaking me out. Rudi had done a great job of putting away money so he would be prepared for the moment he could create a home with his wife. But as I saw our savings account dwindle with every purchase, I couldn't help but fear we would wind up bankrupt. I started to let that fear consume me and cause all kinds of stress and anxiety, which took the fun out of what should have been a joyful, expansive experience of creating our first home together. Finally, Rudi lovingly pointed out that I was viewing our bank account as if the coffers would never refill, as if this were the *only* money we would ever have. He believed there would always be more.

In my heart, I knew he was right, and I went to work shifting this belief. At first, it felt forced, as I didn't fully trust in this "universal flow of abundance" as Rudi did. But as the weeks and months passed, new opportunities and sources of revenue appeared. Before I knew it, all the money we had spent on our home had been replaced and even increased. I regretted the weeks I had spent stressing about the unknown state of our finances—what a waste of time and joy!

I would love to tell you that this experience changed everything for me and that my limiting beliefs about money were magically transformed, but that wouldn't be accurate. It was the *first* of hundreds of opportunities to heal my money wounds and lack mindset.

Over the next few years, I came up against all of my conscious and subconscious beliefs about money, including but not limited to: *Money is evil. Rich people are sinners. Wanting nice things is greedy. I don't deserve a lot of money. Making money requires tremendous hard work and sacrifice. More money means more problems. I'm not smart enough to invest or handle my finances. There's not enough money to go around. I can't charge too much for my services. I need to save every penny I make. If I leave my job, we'll go broke.* Yep, I was forced to face every possible misbelief about money that has ever existed. Good times.

But let me tell you, on the other side of all those lack- and fear-based illusions is *freedom.*

I now know that money is an energy that flows as readily as oxygen. I believe the Universe always supports me to manifest whatever desire comes through me. I know that making money can be easy, fun, and creative. I know that I am on the Universe's payroll, and if I follow my heart and do what lights me up, the money will follow.

As you choose to align with your purpose and live a life of meaning, you will have to trust that the Universe has your back and will continue to invest in your dreams. But first, you must understand how you bought into lack in the first place.

THE TRUTH ABOUT LACK

We are taught from a young age that lack is a real thing. There are too many people on this planet and not enough resources to go around, right?

What if I told you there is *always* enough? The Universe doesn't create lack—we do. It's an illusion born from another familiar illusion: fear. The Universe is limitless. It's our belief in limited resources that causes perceived shortages.

Considering the alarming poverty rate, the number of malnourished children, and the homeless epidemic, I know this concept can be a hard pill to swallow. It's hard to understand why any soul would choose to be born into or experience a situation of lack; however, from a soul perspective, it offers enormous potential for growth and expansion. Those who don't have a lot must muster the courage, strength, and faith to move forward and create a better existence.

I urge you to take a second to ponder this: What if the Universe is unlimited and we've all been under a potent spell called "there's not enough"?

In the Bible, there's a powerful story of Jesus demonstrating this fundamental truth when he fed five thousand people using a couple small baskets of fish and bread. Remarkably, the baskets continued to fill, even after thousands of hands hungrily reached in for more. Whether this actually happened or was included in the Bible as a powerful metaphor for life, I'm not sure, but does it matter?

We create with our beliefs, thoughts, emotions, words, and actions. This means that if we genuinely believe lack exists, that is what we will continue to perpetuate and ultimately create in our realities. Lack is a misconception that has pervaded our conscious and subconscious minds for centuries—a cycle that needs to be ended, not by a few, but by many.

I want you to take a second, close your eyes, and imagine that you just received an official notice in the mail stating that you've been permanently added to the Universe's payroll and that your needs will be met for the rest of your life. You will have more than enough money, food, security, and resources to provide for your family and fulfill your purpose.

What does that feel like? Do you feel a sense of relief?

With this newfound knowledge, would you act differently? Of course you would! With all your needs taken care of, you could then relax, and when you encounter someone in need, say, "Here, have mine. I've got plenty and more on the way."

We must learn to see the world as a place with plenty for everyone. Just because you can't see how it's humanly possible that there will ever be enough dollars, homes, food, and schools for everyone, this doesn't mean that it doesn't exist.

When did you last receive a bill from the sun for the heat it provides? And what about the rain? When's the last time you walked through an untouched forest and thought, *If only there were more plants*?

The nature of the Universe is abundance, expansion, and growth, and free resources are everywhere to support that. Why would *you* be any different?

HOW CAN YOU INCREASE THE FINANCIAL FLOW?

#1. Upgrade your beliefs about money

Are you currently struggling with financial abundance and experiencing stress and anxiety about money? If so, you can change your situation, but first, you'll need to release your limiting beliefs about money.

As discussed earlier in this chapter, I had pages of misbeliefs from my childhood, which were validated and strengthened as I got older. These beliefs formed an energetic dam and needed to be removed so the Universal energies of abundance could flow freely to me.

I took inventory of all the beliefs I was conscious of, writing them down in my journal. I then investigated them one by one, allowing myself to go back to the first time I had the thought, where it came from.

I then determined whether these beliefs were accurate and worth holding on to. Spoiler alert: None of them made the cut.

Next, I rewrote a new belief in each one's place and started stacking evidence in their favor, even looking at other people's experiences to demonstrate their truth. Some of these beliefs were easy to shift, but others held on for dear life. It's scary to let go of the ideas and opinions you have carried for a long time as they form the mental structure by which you make sense of the world.

But in my case, the opposite was true. I felt empowered, supported, and *free*. Sometimes, the old beliefs will still pop up in my inner narrative, but I can quickly recognize them and shoo them away.

What's your relationship with money? Do you like it, or do you cringe and want to cover your eyes whenever you check your bank balance? If money were a person, what personality characteristics would you assign to it? Is it a male or female? Are they friendly or bitchy? Are they stuck up and petty, or powerful, ethical, and generous?

These questions might seem silly, but it's a quick way to get a good read on how you *feel* about money—and how you feel is a symptom of what you believe.

Only you can change *your* beliefs. You must take the first step in faith. What's the worst thing that could happen when you question a long-held opinion of how the Universe works when it doles out money? The worst thing would be for you to find out your belief is, in fact, correct—so really, you have nothing to lose!

One idea that has been particularly life-changing for me is that the Universe can and will send you financial blessings from an infinite number of unexpected sources. It's so easy to get caught in the trap of believing your job is your source of income when it's just one option in a sea of investors.

While yes, the Universe might be supporting you through a single job right now, that might shift and change—to the degree that you will lift that restrictive belief. Be open to the idea that you will receive funds in any way the Universe sees fit, and watch what happens.

Rudi and I have received money from unexpected tax refunds, free trips to exotic locations, new clients who have come out of nowhere ready to pay in full, and opportunities to pay less for utilities, which, in essence, is like a pay raise!

Repeat after me, "I am open to receiving *all* the blessings of financial abundance from any source and at any time. May the loving Universe pour all its blessings on me, and I will receive with an open and grateful heart."

#2. Become abundance

As discussed in Chapter 4: Manifest Your New Vision, you don't manifest what you want; you manifest what you are.

You can desire more money all day long. However, if you still embody the energy of poverty, you will get more poverty. The outer world is just a reflection of who you are and who you believe yourself to be. You must become abundant before you can experience more abundance.

You can use many tools and tactics to do this, including creating a habit of writing out your affirmations to shift your inner narrative. For instance, start your day by writing out, "I am abundant in all ways" or, "I am financially supported by the Universe and magnetizing unlimited financial abundance."

A common question is: If you've never experienced wealth or abundance, how do you embody it? Well, I bet you have experienced abundance in some areas of your life. Maybe you've always had an abundance of fulfilling friendships, an abundance of love for your children, or an abundance of health.

Identify one area of your life you feel abundant in and imagine it in your mind. How does it feel? Does your body feel relaxed and at peace with no thoughts or worry about whether there will be enough or if it will all go away? Do you feel confident and joyful?

Take a minute to connect to that feeling for a few minutes, and then, holding on to the feeling, transfer back to an image of yourself experiencing financial wealth. Spend time borrowing the energy from an area of your life that is *in the flow* until it starts to become your dominant energy in every area of your life.

#3. Gratitude

Practicing gratitude is one of the quickest ways to shift your energetic frequency and receive more abundance. It's virtually impossible to feel grateful and fearful simultaneously, so a daily gratitude practice is a powerful way to open the floodgates for more financial abundance to come your way. What you focus on expands, so the more you focus on the things in your life that you are grateful for, the more things you will receive to be thankful for.

What if you woke up tomorrow and all that was left was what you're grateful for? What would still be there? Would you wish you had expressed gratitude for your coffee machine brewing hot coffee for you every morning? Would your car still be waiting for you in the driveway? What about your husband? Your kids? Your health?

You have reason to express gratitude for everything in your life, even the things that appear negative or challenging, because they provide you with learning and growth. You are unbelievably blessed. So, if you're feeling out of sorts, anxious, stressed, or panicked about your finances, get out that gratitude journal and go to town, my friend.

#4. Give

How often have you wanted to donate money or give something to someone else but stopped and thought, *If I give, then I won't have enough*? Come on, be honest, we've all been there!

I once read about the ancient spiritual Law of Ten, which stuck with me. This law states that what you give, you receive back tenfold. Whether you're giving money, a smile to a stranger, a nasty text to an ex, or cutting in line at the DMV, you will get it back, in some form, times ten.

I experienced this firsthand in college. I was approached by a homeless man on my way into the grocery store, and he asked if I could give him money. I hesitated but reached into my purse to see if I had any cash. When I opened my wallet, I saw a single ten-dollar bill, which was a lot of money to me at the time, but at that point I couldn't just give him nothing. So, I took a deep breath and handed it to him with a smile. He thanked me profusely and went on his way.

On my way out of the grocery store, I saw a crumpled bill on the ground near my car's driver side door. I bent down to pick it up and quickly realized it was a hundred-dollar bill. Ten dollars times ten equals one hundred. What a coincidence, right? It just so happens this was not the only time this spiritual law has shown itself in my life.

A few years after that experience, I was working in a sales position overseas. I had very little overhead, so I was able to start my first savings account. I learned that a friend was going through a tough time and was in trouble financially. She never once asked me for money or even alluded to it, but I kept getting the nudge to leave an envelope with cash in it for her. I went to the bank and withdrew the $5,000 I had put into savings, sealed it in an envelope, and left it hidden in a place I knew she would find.

That financial gift was, and still is, a lot of money to me. It took a lot of courage and faith to follow that nudge, but it felt so good when I did, as if she'd given me a gift instead of the other way around.

A month later, I was offered a sales opportunity in a different region that historically hadn't produced a lot of revenue. I reluctantly said yes and reminded myself that it was temporary. From day one, sales closed quickly, and the money began to flow. I felt like I was in a perpetual state of good luck. At the end of that sales contract, I had exceeded all my targets and earned more than $50,000 in commission. I could replace the money I had taken from savings and then some! My unconditional gift of $5,000 quickly multiplied and returned to me in a beautiful, loving, and abundant way.

Let me clarify: It won't always come back to you in the same form or timeframe. For instance, I could have won a trip or received a promotion instead of cash. If you were to donate food to a shelter, instead of receiving a bag of groceries in return, you might get a loving, thoughtful letter from your spouse that warms your heart, or your friend might take you out to dinner.

The Universe is creative when it comes to gift-giving.

#5. Receive

For many people, it's easier to give than it is to receive. While giving doesn't require you to recognize your self-worth, receiving does. Many people suffer from a self-worth deficit.

Your birthright is abundance, and the Universe is waiting to bestow your inheritance to support you in fulfilling your purpose. There's nothing you have to do to deserve what is divinely yours. All that is required is to claim and embody the belief that you *are* abundant and worthy of all the blessings coming your way.

Deep down, do you believe you are worthy to receive what you desire? When a friend offers to help, do you say yes or do you thank them but decline the assistance, not wanting to be a bother? How about when a surprise opportunity comes your way that could lead to more money—do you excitedly accept, or do you turn it down?

My challenge to you is to start accepting the small things first. Allow others to give to you, knowing it's benefiting them just as much as you, if not more. Then, when the lucrative opportunity lands on your doorstep, you will trust that you are worthy and receive it with open arms.

The Universe we live in is unlimited in abundance and does not withhold its blessings unless you obstruct it with beliefs and fears of lack. You will be supported in the ideal way and at the perfect time with the resources you need to survive and thrive.

Aligning with your purpose will steer you down unknown paths, which will require a strong faith that you will be guided and supported financially.

PUTTING IT INTO PRACTICE

Think back to a time when you unexpectedly received financial abundance from a source other than your employer or profession. Write down the memories as they come of the gifts you've received from loved ones—free meals from friends, buy-one-get-one-free shoe sales, surprise refunds you received in the mail, or an offer to babysit your kids for free.

Make your list as long as possible, and don't stop till you've filled the page.

Don't you see how abundant you are? Give thanks for every entry on your list, and fill yourself with positive expectations for all the gifts yet to come!

Chapter 15

NEVER STOP GROWING

Life itself is your teacher, and you are in
a constant state of learning.

—Bruce Lee

I LOVE TO LEARN. SOME might argue I am a bit addicted. I still wake up early and stay up late to dig into the latest nonfiction book that caught my eye on my weekly visits to Barnes & Noble. While I've always been a bookworm, my ravenous appetite for studying books on spirituality, metaphysics, energy, and personal development started in my early twenties. I didn't question why; I just wanted to do it.

I discovered that with each book, I learned something that could improve my life experience. Sometimes, I gained a deeper understanding of my purpose in the world or picked up a cool manifestation tool or a strategy for improving my relationships. It was virtually impossible for me to absorb *all* the information I was consuming. But even internalizing one valuable takeaway, new philosophy, belief, action, or way of being made it time well spent.

What I now know is that my natural love for reading and consuming personal development texts was no accident. It came from my inner knowing that someday I would need this information. I was being qualified, and this was my training. Every book was perfectly timed for what I needed to learn next, as if I were following a pre-ordained curriculum. Sometimes, it felt almost magical, especially when a book fell off the bookstore shelf in front of me or I received a book in the mail from someone who felt inspired to buy it for me one day.

I often conversed with friends, family, and coworkers who would share with me problems they were facing in their lives. In divine order, I would have just read a book on that topic and be able to offer insight and actions they could take to resolve the problem. I began to understand that this knowledge was for more than just collecting and hoarding. I was supposed to share it with others when I felt inspired.

The more I opened to sharing, the more frequently opportunities came to do so, and each experience left me feeling invigorated and lit up from the inside out. I actively sought out meaningful conversations and loved offering advice and providing a safe space for people to share.

As a high-level business executive, I would find myself coaching business clients in what was originally on the calendar as a sales conversation. Colleagues from other departments knocked on my office door to ask if they could chat about their personal issues. Those moments of sharing my knowledge and wisdom with someone in need became my favorite part of my day. In hindsight, I was given the opportunity to be a spiritual teacher and coach before I desired to make it my life's work.

As I became aware of my purpose and life vision, I quickly realized there was *so* much I did not know. I had been on a DIY education plan, and it had worked for me so far. It was affordable and effective. But I still had some blocks and negative patterns, like procrastination and perfectionism, that I hadn't been able to break through on my own, and I knew I needed help.

One day, I found an online video of a successful high-performance coach sharing tips and tools to up-level your life and achieve your goals. I felt drawn to her and wanted to hear more. Something inside said, "This is the next step." So, I scheduled a call with her to see if she could help. My call with her was unbelievable! With every ounce of my being, I knew that she could help move me forward. But holy moly, when she told me the price of her program—$15,000—I almost had a heart attack.

While I had paid off a whopping $60,000 college loan in my twenties, besides buying books and a few online courses that cost less than $100 each, I had yet to invest much money in my continued education. Committing to spending five figures on a coach without guaranteeing it would result in anything seemed irresponsible and downright crazy. So, I politely declined and decided to go back to figuring it out on my own.

Fast-forward a year. I was still chasing my tail. The thought of contacting that coach had crossed my mind hundreds of times, but I repeatedly squelched it because I could not justify the cost.

When I told Rudi about it, he responded, "If this is what you feel you need to do, then do it! What's the worst thing that can happen? You could stay in the exact place you are now. Or, you can succeed and feel more empowered in your life." Then he added, "I believe in you, Anniston." And there it was. He believed in me, and I *didn't*. That needed to change.

That day, I hired a coach. I showed up weekly, followed her advice, did the work, and committed to action. She helped me get clear on my vision and held me accountable for moving forward, even when I was afraid. This was the key to breaking out of my old pattern of self-sabotage.

You will always be a work in progress—the learning literally never ends. When one lesson is ending, another is beginning. In reality, you will never be fully enlightened and know all there is to know. Earth is not just a planet. It is a *school.*

WELCOME TO EARTH SCHOOL

From your first breath until your last, you are enrolled in the most advanced school in the Universe—Earth School.

Unlike the traditional education system where you are taught curriculum in a classroom setting, your Earth School classes take place in every moment, experience, interaction, thought, and action.

What's the point of all this learning? It is to remind you of the truth of who you really are.

I believe we are souls created from the same source, unlimited in our capacity to create, expand, and love. But we forget our divinity—who we are, what we are, and how we're meant to serve. While your physical senses are limited in their ability to recognize evidence of your true birthright, your inner self *knows* and will guide you to the very things, people, and experiences that will trigger those memories.

At Earth School, the stakes are high. Will you remember and live a life of ease and joy? Or will you stay in forgetfulness and keep the negative emotions that come with believing that you are a victim of life's circumstances? You get to remember your power, that love is your natural state, and fear is an illusion. You get to remember you are an eternal soul, and there are no endings (e.g., death), just transitions to new beginnings.

The fact that you are reading this book and have made it to the last chapter tells me there is something within you that will resonate with this truth. You must have a flicker of remembrance about the truth of who you are.

Your authentic self wants to take a more significant role in your life. This is a milestone along your life education journey. It means you have passed mandatory tests and initiations, wrestling with and answering the hard questions: Will you live a life that others expect of you, or will you live the one you desire? Will you remain a victim of your fear of judgment and rejection, or will you move through them to see that they are all illusions? Huge congrats—those classes are damn hard to pass, but they come with the greatest rewards!

Let me share some of my biggest takeaways on navigating my way through Earth School, at least so far, because, just like yours, my education is endless.

#1. Embrace being a lifelong student

It is common to believe that just one book, course, conference, coach, or mentor will provide you the holy grail of understanding and enlightenment. As teachers, our egos love to think what we share will be *the* thing that will change our students' lives forever. But that is not how Earth School is designed.

Imagine you are a giant jigsaw puzzle separated into thousands of pieces. With every piece placed, the picture becomes clearer, making it easier to identify the next one. That is an excellent metaphor for your life education journey. You might reach points in your life when you can't imagine adding another piece to your puzzle. Yet, another truth will emerge, and it will make your life even more surprising and beautiful than it was before.

Oprah Winfrey has been quoted as saying, "Dear Lord, please don't teach me anything today," which I still think is hilarious. Some days, that is exactly how I feel, especially in challenging times. What you have learned up to this moment has gotten you where you are today. Embrace being a lifelong student. When you know better, you do better. When you expand your understanding and beliefs about yourself, everything in your outer world will shift too. Everything that has ever happened and will ever happen is *for* you. It is your assigned curriculum, preparing you for your destiny.

#2. Teachers come in many forms

Teachers come in many forms, and they're not always the person standing on a stage, writing a book, or giving a lecture in a classroom. In one moment, the teacher is the bird singing outside your window, reminding you to pause, be present, and embrace joy. In another, the teacher is your snarky boss, teaching you to see through his bravado and know that his insults and impatience reflect how he feels inside. In another, the teacher shifts into your six-year-old daughter, who calls you out for breaking your promise to get home from work to play dolls with her. This allows you to practice and understand the importance of keeping your word. Wherever the student goes, there will always be a teacher present.

What if everything you can physically see outside yourself is a teacher? What if every character and prop appears in the scene at just the right time to teach you something? You need to recognize that even those relationships that have broken your heart into a million pieces somehow served your growth.

Our teachers can change forms at any given moment, and they can also come and go. Can you imagine being enrolled in first grade your entire life, having only one teacher to inform you of everything you need to know? That would be impossible! I have seen many people hold too tightly to one philosophy, teaching, or teacher because it served them at one point in their lives. If you fail to listen to your intuition, you will stall your growth and personal evolution. However, if you listen and trust, you will always be guided to the next best teacher on your path.

You will also be drawn to different interests for specific purposes. For example, there was a five-year period in which I studied and became a master-certified numerologist. I was obsessed with learning about the energy of numbers and had a growing list of clients who came to me for readings. I thought I would do this forever!

Learning numerology and providing readings was exactly what I was meant to do then. But eventually, the joy it yielded started to wane, and my interests moved on to other things. I was drawn to other advanced healing modalities as well as coaching. Here's the thing: I use *all* the knowledge I've accumulated to serve others, including providing numerology readings to my colleagues, friends, family, and coaching clients. There are no wasted moments and experiences. Don't feel guilty and ashamed about walking away from something that no longer lights you up or feels right. It was not a mistake, and it will continue to serve you and others in some way in the future.

#3. Ask for your next assignment

Eventually, you will be ready to participate actively in your life education. This means you are no longer learning by default but *on purpose.*

The true nature of your soul is expansion, which is why progress is one of the keys to sustained and consistent happiness. When you stop learning, growing, and moving toward something greater, you become clouded and sick like a swampy, bacteria-infested green pond.

One way to become a co-creator of your education is to ask the following questions:

- What is my next area of opportunity?
- What is showing up for me right now that is triggering or testing me?
- What am I interested in learning more about right now?
- What do I need to become or learn to achieve my goal?

Rather than wait like a sitting duck for the Universe to bring you the next step in your growth, *ask* for it! It is a Universal law that if you ask a question, the answer will appear. But the answer will rarely come in the way you think it will. Be open-minded and present, and pay attention! There have been times I was driving by a bookstore en route to an appointment and I felt like an invisible force took control of my hands, steering me into the parking lot. Of course, the book I took home was the answer to the very question I had been asking.

You get to have fun with this! The Universe does have the most brilliant sense of humor. I once asked in a meditation if I was being supported in writing a book. When I opened my eyes, a white feather had landed on the top of my laptop, sitting right in front of me.

It is important to note that your next cut will not necessarily be someone else's. I must remember this often. I will finish a book and immediately transfer it to Rudi's bedside table, proclaiming, "Oh my gosh, you must read this!" Sometimes he agrees, and other times not. That's okay because some other "teacher" might be center-stage with him at the moment.

In that case, he is either not ready or not a match for the information I have just consumed. We are all at different points in our journey of remembering. Wherever someone is, behind you or ahead, honor it. They are exactly where they need to be. Attempting to force someone to understand something they are not ready for is ineffective. They will be ready when they are ready.

#4. Be willing to invest in you

Bestselling author Robin Sharma states, "Investing in yourself is the best investment you will ever make. It will not only improve your life, but it will also improve the lives of all those around you."

If you find yourself at a point in your life where you want to create positive shifts and improvements, the most effective way to do that is to invest in a mentor or coach to help you get there. It took me a long time to feel worthy and confident enough to hire a coach to guide me to a specific result, but now I actively seek them out.

When you invest your money in something, it is like putting a stake in the sand, proclaiming to the Universe that this is what you value. Will that $200 pair of high heels result in a more abundant, inspired life? If so, go on with your bad self, sister! But if not, where else could you invest that money that will help you feel better, do better, and be better?

There is not one Olympic athlete who doesn't have an army of coaches who helped them get there. The same applies to every United States president, famous actor, legendary CEO, and hall-of-fame quarterback. I remember watching a documentary on Tom Brady, which recounted how he spent his off-season working with a coach to perfect his throw *after* winning the Super Bowl.

These legendary individuals know that to continue to up their game, they need to seek out people who can help them get there. You will save a ton of stress, money, and time by allowing someone to show you how to do something versus trying to figure it out alone! They will also be able to point out your blind spots (because we all have them) and any negative stories you have about why you can't or won't achieve something. They will stretch you out of your comfort zone and hold you accountable for consistent action.

I recommend looking at your budget and starting to carve out funds that you can put into investing in yourself and your purpose. Whether it's $5 or $5,000 a month, just taking that action will tell the Universe you are serious and will amplify your intention. Rudi and I invest a lot of money in our personal development every year. Whether it is on private coaching, online courses, or attending conferences—we know we wouldn't be living the unbelievable life we are without all those experiences. We are always reaching for our next cut.

Here are a few tips for choosing a mentor, coach, or program:

1. First and foremost, ask yourself if this person or program *feels* right.
2. Find someone who has achieved the very results you desire.
3. Make sure your values and beliefs align with theirs.
4. Commit to getting the most out of any opportunity while working with someone (e.g., attend every call, ask lots of questions, and get into action).
5. If you want a coach but are afraid you can't afford it, ask the Universe, "What would it take for me to afford a coach that can move me forward?" And, when you get the inspired answer, *act*!

#5. Act

Knowledge is potential power. It's when you act on what you have learned and change your behavior that you can benefit from the knowledge. If you read a book, hire a coach, or take a class, be clear on your intention before starting. What do you most want to gain? What area of your life do you most want to improve? Then, commit to completing the assignments. Don't just skip over the exercises, thinking they are a waste of time.

I can't tell you how many people I have met who said, "I didn't get anything out of that course." But, when I asked if they put into action anything they learned, they admitted they didn't. You will never actually change until you embody a new belief or way of being. This is another reason why it is crucial to invest real money into your personal development. You will be less likely to give up and half-ass it. The money you invest is for the result you seek!

You need to be willing to go all in, not just when you are on the call with your coach or sitting at the conference. It is the moments in between when real learning occurs, as you get to practice what you have learned and embody positive behavior.

This book is not the end-all, be-all of living a more joyful, abundant life and fulfilling your unique purpose in this lifetime. It will be one impactful piece of the puzzle that will assist you on your journey, but there will be many more. You do not need to know everything to start because you will learn as you go, and the Universe will support you.

You will *never* know it all, so there is no reason to delay creating positive changes in your life. Become a willing participant on your journey, trusting that with each experience, you are being prepared for the next. Seek out teachers and be ready to receive those who cross your path, trusting they have an important message to share. Remind yourself that everything in your reality has been orchestrated to help you learn something, so forgive quickly. Don't linger too long on each lesson; another one is waiting just around the corner.

PUTTING IT INTO PRACTICE

Take a few moments to anchor the information in this book. What are the two or three main ideas that you have taken away? What aha moments did they trigger? What new ideas have formed because of them?

Now, copy into your journal the following question: "What would it take for me to embody these new ideas so they positively affect my life?"

Write down three to five action steps you can take for each one and commit to doing them with a deadline and milestone steps.

CLOSE

THE UNIVERSE IS HIRING.

There's a position available right now that only *you* were born to fill. This role perfectly suits you and offers incredible benefits—unlimited abundance, meaning, freedom, fulfillment, joy, and wholeness.

The requirements for this position include showing up every day as the most authentic version of yourself, following the guidance of your heart, acknowledging and honing your unique gifts and talents, remaining open to where you are guided to serve, trusting that whatever is in front of you is your assignment for that day, letting go of the need to be defined by a title, committing to manifesting the dreams and desires you carry, and pursuing what will bring you joy.

This position is not just a job—it's a *way of being.*

Your willingness to fulfill this role will align you with the most extraordinary path available. This path will lead to your highest expression and potential in this lifetime. It will allow you to fulfill your heroic mission and experience everything your heart desires.

You are being called to align with your purpose.

All interested applicants must *apply within.*

ACKNOWLEDGMENTS

FIRST AND FOREMOST, I'D LIKE to thank my husband, Rudi, for supporting me through every step of this journey. Your love, encouragement, and unwillingness to allow me to give up on my dreams is why this book exists. I love doing life with you.

I want to thank the fantastic support of the KN Literary team—specifically Shannon Azzato Stephens and Lauren DeSanto—for sharing their editing genius with me and this project. I also want to thank the incredible Greenleaf Book Group Press publishing team—especially Dee Kerr, Adrianna Hernandez, Sally Garland, Aaron Teel, Sheila Parr, and Tenyia Lee. Thank you for leading me by the hand throughout this process and showing up with integrity, honesty, and purpose every step of the way.

To my Effy Jewelry family, you are truly extraordinary. I now know what working for a supportive, heart-centered, purpose-driven company looks like. My experience working with this organization inspired me to write this book—it turns out that work can be truly fulfilling when you're encouraged to share your unique gifts and allowed to shine.

To my beautiful and fierce colleagues and soul sisters Shanèe, Jennifer, and Jenna—thank you for creating a safe space for me to show up, be seen, and be *me*. I love you.

Special thanks to my mother, Glenda Hovenkamp, who has been my constant cheerleader on this writing journey, reading each chapter as I finished, asking probing questions, and encouraging me to dig deeper. Mom, I cherish you.

To my little sister and talented designer Sarah Hovenkamp, thank you for sharing your creative genius and brilliant designs. You gave this book a soul; I will be eternally grateful for that.

Thank you to our amazing InPowered Life community. Your willingness to learn, grow, and expand reminds me daily to do the same.

And finally, thank you to my beautiful children, Brady and Ali Olivia, for never letting me forget my promise to take you to Universal Studios when I publish this book. Let's do this!

ABOUT THE AUTHOR

ANNISTON BLAIR RIEKSTINS IS A high-performance coach, spiritual teacher, motivational speaker, and high-level executive. She regularly hosts live training and virtual workshops, teaching corporate professionals how to up-level their mindset and align with their unique purpose.

Anniston is the co-host of the InPowered Life podcast and co-founder of InPower University, an online platform featuring courses and coaching for busy professionals.

Anniston lives in Wilmington, North Carolina, with her husband, two kids, and two dachshunds.

Find out more at www.annistonriekstins.com.